You Can Cook This!

You Can Cook This!

Simple, satisfying, sustainable veg recipes

Max La Manna

EBURY PRESS

5 Leafy Greens & Cruciferous   140

Cauliflower
Broccoli
Herbs

6 Fungi & Alliums   172

Mushrooms
Onion
Garlic

7 Non-dairy   204

Milk
Yoghurt

8 Fruits   222

Apple
Banana
Berries
Citrus

9 Leftovers   238

Introduction

If you ask me what I love the most, I would say to you without hesitation – food (really sorry to my wife: she knows this already, and she's a close second). I have never been shy to talk about food nor my passion for wasting less of it.

First and foremost, my love of food means that I simply enjoy cooking and eating it, and I hate seeing it wasted. However, I grew up in the USA, which is without a doubt one of the most wasteful countries in the world, and its throw-away food culture is no exception.

It's not just pre-packaged fast and cheap food that is treated as disposable: the same ethos is found in high-end restaurants, too. During my time trying to make it as an actor, I worked at an array of restaurants in Los Angeles and New York City, including one with a Michelin star. Food waste was rife at all of them. It pained me.

Once I admitted defeat against my acting aspirations, I turned my focus to championing the food we already have in our fridges and cupboards, and finding exciting new ways to cook the meals we crave the most. I did this in person by hosting dinners for friends, corporate events and demonstrations, and then later on a digital scale, creating content that is accessible and easy to follow for as many people as possible.

The recipes I've created are here to inspire, excite and transform the way you cook, store and save food. You may be someone who cooks every day, or perhaps you're someone who wants to learn or cook more – whoever you are, whatever your motivation, this book is a practical guide, showing you how to develop and cook delicious, simple dishes with the food you already have in your kitchen.

You Can Cook This! – and you probably should! Get in the kitchen right now, explore your fridge and cupboards, uncover the neglected and forgotten ingredients – as long as it's safe to eat and there isn't mould growing on it – and cook your way through these pages. You'll see how effortless it is to create meals using what you already have, and what's more, they'll save you money and time.

Why I Wrote This Cookbook

Before we start cooking, I need to say a BIG thank you to those of you who follow me on social media. I asked you for ideas and inspiration; you may recall the question boxes on my Instagram stories that said: 'Tell me the food you waste the most', and from this simple question, I had tens of thousands of responses. Collecting the data, I've narrowed it down to the top 30 most-wasted ingredients in your homes. I don't think you're going to be surprised by the focus-led ingredients in this cookbook – you'll already be familiar with most of them. However, I think you may be encouraged by how easy it is to cook these recipes and waste less food.

How This Cookbook Works

It's easier than ever to cook mouth-watering dishes for yourself and your loved ones. This is how it works: all you need is to find an ingredient you want to cook, head to the chapter with said ingredient, and there you'll find delicious, easy-to-cook recipes to choose from. You'll find further inspiration in the index (page 276). These recipes are designed to encourage you to use the entire vegetable, grain or fruit so that there's no half-cut, rogue piece of onion or bagged salad wilting and rotting away in your fridge.

In this book, there are classics with a twist like my Cauliflower Ragù (page 146), hearty meals such as Romesco Risotto (page 108), fan favourites like Tofu Butter 'Chicken' (page 124) and Crispy Smashed Potatoes (page 36), indulgent sweet recipes, such as Salted Chocolate, Peanut Butter and Tahini Brownies (page 219) and Carrot Pecan Cake and Orange Drizzle (page 46), comfort food, such as Beetroot Bucatini (page 30) or One-pan Lasagna (page 84) and finger-licking snacks – don't miss my Spicy Baked Cauliflower Wings (page 148) and Loaded Nachos (page 19)!

There's a disproportionate amount of pressure placed on personal responsibility to create less waste in the world. The majority of this pressure should be redirected and placed on the world's top 100 most-polluting corporations – who are responsible for 71 per cent of greenhouse gas emissions. Not all individuals have the privilege, time and access to forgo plastic packaging and cook every meal from scratch. With that said, I have first-hand experience of how individual change – with the planet in mind – can benefit our mental health and sense of purpose and community. The more of us aboard this ship, the more positive change we can make.

Enjoy cooking, sharing and eating delicious food,

— Max

Everyone Is Welcome at the Table

This cookbook is a celebration of food. No matter what your dietary preference is. Everyone is welcome to the table. No discrimination, no judgement. What I love most about how I cook is that everyone can eat it (depending on dietary restrictions, of course).

Plant-based equivalents of butter and popular cheeses such as cheddar, feta, mozzarella and parmesan have become easier to find in supermarkets, along with an array of non-dairy milks, yoghurts and creams. Feel free to experiment, or use dairy products if you prefer.

All of the recipes in this book have been tested with plant-based ingredients, as that's how I like to eat.

In the Kitchen

You have found yourself...in the kitchen. For me, the kitchen has always taken centre stage. When I was growing up, it was the hub of our home and now, as an adult, it's where I spend most of my time. If I'm ever at a party, you can always find me in the kitchen. They say we sleep for one-third of our lives; I probably spend more than half my waking life in the kitchen (as I write this, I am in my kitchen).

The kitchen stores food and produces meals. It can be a well-oiled machine or it can be chaos. My kitchen is also my office, so I like to keep it in tip-top shape and clutter-free. What I'm talking about here is how you store your food. Quite simply, it can make or break your meals, and your bank account.

I'm often asked on social media and in person what easy steps we can all take to waste less food. Here are some actions to take to waste a little less food at home:

Make a list before shopping

Do a quick inventory of your fridge and cupboard and see which foods you already have on hand.

Cook

I know it seems obvious, but 40 per cent of food waste is coming from unused produce in the home. Cook the food you already have, find a recipe (perhaps in this book) and start cooking.

Save your leftovers

Keep them in a sealed container either in your fridge or freezer and eat them the next day or later in the week.

Store food properly (see page 10)

Use technology and donate food: there are apps and charities where you can donate food or pick up food from others in your community.

Compost

Food doesn't belong in landfills. Did you know it takes 25 years for a head of lettuce to decompose in a landfill? Whereas if composted properly it would take 30–90 days and provide rich nutrients to the soil. Which of these sounds better to you? If you don't already have a food waste collection, either build a compost heap at home or contact your local council and find out about food waste recycling.

How to Store Food

When you think of storing food, what comes to mind? Do you imagine wrapping your dinner leftovers, putting them in the fridge and calling it a day? All food can be classified under three groups; perishable, semi-perishable and staple.

Perishable foods

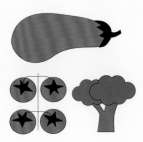

This includes many raw fruits and vegetables – and for those who eat them, meat, dairy and eggs. To store these foods for any length of time, they need to be held at the correct temperature. As a rule, the interior temperature of a fridge can vary between 2 and 5˚C, but check with your country's health department for more accurate advice.

Semi-perishable foods

Flour, grains, dried fruits and seeds, nuts and peanut butter are considered semi-perishable. If optimally stored, in a clean and airtight container kept in a cool, dry place, semi-perishable foods may remain unspoiled for a long time. Freeze them and they can last even longer.

Staple foods

Dried beans, pasta, rice, spices and tinned goods are all non-perishable foods. However, if they are stored incorrectly, they will spoil and lose their quality. Keep these ingredients in cool, dry conditions and out of sunlight. I keep my dried beans, pasta and rice in airtight containers, my spices in sealed jars, and tinned goods in a cupboard out of direct sunlight.

The Fridge

The most common way many of us store produce is in the fridge. Always keep an eye on the temperature of your fridge and avoid overcrowding it. Stuffing your fridge with food can impact the air circulation inside, meaning that food can spoil even more rapidly. Every two weeks, take five minutes to go through your fridge and see what belongs and what doesn't. I like doing this because sometimes – even for me – food gets shoved to the back and is lost forever. For a more detailed overview of how to get the most out of your food through proper storage, I've included a table at the back of the book (page 270) that covers all the key ingredients used in this book.

- Fruits with stones, such as peaches and plums, should be placed in a closed paper bag until ripe, then kept in the fridge.

- Keep tomatoes at room temperature only if they'll be eaten within 1–2 days – otherwise, they go in the fridge. They like their space, so don't overcrowd them, and place them stem side down.

The Freezer

Along with pre-frozen foods, freeze leftovers, bread and herbs. Before freezing, wrap and label food.

The Pantry/Kitchen Cupboards

These should be cool, dry and, ideally, dark, to provide optimal storage conditions for pasta, rice and other grains, dried beans and lentils, flour, sugar, dried fruits, nuts and seeds, peanut butter and tinned goods.

- Keep potatoes in a cool, dark place.

- Onions and garlic also like a cool, dark place, but not in the same space as the potatoes. Store them separately.

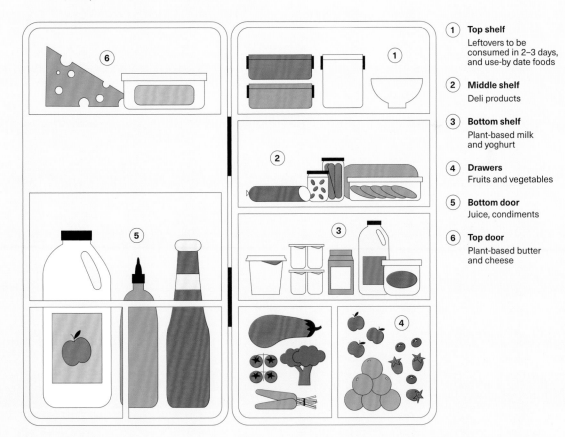

1. **Top shelf**
   Leftovers to be consumed in 2–3 days, and use-by date foods

2. **Middle shelf**
   Deli products

3. **Bottom shelf**
   Plant-based milk and yoghurt

4. **Drawers**
   Fruits and vegetables

5. **Bottom door**
   Juice, condiments

6. **Top door**
   Plant-based butter and cheese

How to Clean Vegetables and Fruits

- Always wash produce before preparing; it's usually best to do this just before you use it.

- Remove and compost the outer leaves of leafy greens, such as cabbage and lettuce, if they seem like they've had better days.

- Wash your hands with warm, soapy water, then gently rub produce under running water. Use a vegetable brush on firmer produce.

- If you're worried about dirt or bugs, soak produce for a few minutes in a mix of 10 parts water to 1 part white vinegar. Salt can also be added to the mix.

Using Leftovers

Or what I like to call Tomorrow's Lunch. Please try not to throw away your leftovers. They often taste even better the next day!

- Cool leftovers as quickly as possible once they've been cooked, ideally within two hours.

- Divide leftovers into portions, then chill or freeze.

- If chilling, use within three days.

- Always defrost leftovers completely, either in the fridge or on the worktop.

- When defrosted, reheat only once. The more times you cool and reheat food, the higher the risk of food poisoning.

- When reheating food, ensure it reaches 70°C for two minutes to kill off any bacteria.

- For safety and to waste less food, only take out of the freezer what you intend to consume within 24 hours.

Food Labelling, What Does It All Mean?

I have a confession: I was confused by this a few years ago, but once I wrapped my head around it, I finally conquered this confusing labelling system. It's one area that is often overlooked when preventing food waste.

Use-by

The use-by date means that after the date shown the food is deemed by the manufacturer as no longer safe to eat. However, some foods can be eaten after this date if they are frozen before this date. How I like to remember it: use this food before or on this date.

Best-before

Best-before dates are all about the quality. Enjoy this food before or on this date. After this date, it is safe to eat, but may not be at its best. Use your best judgement. Inspect it, smell it, taste a tiny amount of it.

Sell-by

Sell-by dates are to inform the shop to sell this product. This is for the shop only and you can most certainly ignore this, but use your judgement before buying. I like buying sell-by date bread when I see it and freezing it as soon as I get home. It's usually on offer, too!

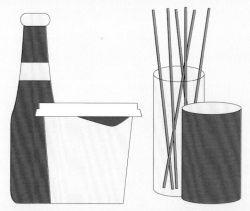

Chop Chop – Simple Preparation to Waste Less Food

In every food preparation, there is some element of 'waste', right? What if I told you I can help you minimise the amount of food that's binned?

At the back of this book (page 270) you will find a simple guide that will show you how to get ahead and waste less by properly prepping all of the key ingredients used in this book. By introducing these small hacks into your food preparation you will reduce food waste, save money and send less to landfills. Prepping ingredients before you start to cook can also save time: you won't need to stop mid-recipe to chop herbs or zest a lemon. Remember:

- Eat the skin. Don't peel potatoes, carrots, apples, pears and kiwis.
- Perk up your water. Add peelings from citrus fruits or cucumber to a jug of cold water.
- Be a seed saver. Bake, toast or fry the seeds from butternut squash and pumpkin.
- Blitz your bread. Freeze breadcrumbs to use in stuffings and toppings.
- Blend it up.
- Add leafy greens to smoothies, blend and freeze herbs, garlic and ginger in ice cube trays.
- Make a veg stock with scraps (page 260).
- Save leftovers to eat tomorrow.
- Keep your fridge clutter-free.
- Use your freezer more often.
- Compost, if you can.
- Don't worry about being perfect.

How to Use This Book

Below the recipes you will often find tips and tricks to help you get the best results and avoid waste. You will also see the following icons:

Serves/Makes	Gives you an idea of how many the dish will feed. That may depend on your appetite, and whether you serve it as a main or side dish.	**Leftovers**	Tells you how long leftovers will keep, covered or wrapped, in the fridge.
Prep Time	This includes chopping but not marinating, chilling or rising times for dough.	**Freezer Friendly**	Tells you how long you can keep leftovers in the freezer.
Cook Time	The amount of time in the oven or on the hob. This may vary depending on the size of the ingredient.	**Gluten Free** **GF**	Tells you that the recipe is entirely gluten free. I have included separate tips on how to make simple swaps if you need a gluten-free option.

1– Root Vegetables

Carrot
Parsnip
Potato
Beetroot

Carrot Lox and Bagel

If you go for a walk in Brooklyn on a Sunday, I'd guess that one in every ten people will have a bagel with smoked salmon and cream cheese in their hands! I teased this recipe on social media and EVERYONE wanted to know how to make it. It's the first time I'm sharing it – and I promise you won't be disappointed! Surprisingly easy to make, carrot strips soften in the marinade, becoming deliciously chewy and it has the perfect balance of smoky spices, mimicking the texture and taste of smoked salmon. Pile it high on a bagel with cream cheese, Pickled Red Onion and capers. What more can you ask for?

4 large carrots
3 tbsp olive oil
1 tbsp rice vinegar
2 tsp liquid smoke
½ tsp smoked paprika
¼ tsp black pepper
pinch of salt

To serve
4 bagels or slices of toast
150–200g cream cheese
Pickled Red Onion (page 267)
capers
finely chopped chives

1   Preheat the oven to 150°C/130°C fan/gas 2. Line a baking sheet with baking parchment.

2   Using a vegetable peeler, peel the carrots into long thin ribbons. Place the ribbons on the baking sheet and bake for 10–12 minutes, until soft. Remove from the oven and set aside to cool.

3   Meanwhile, in a bowl or container, whisk together the remaining ingredients.

4   Add the carrots to the marinade and gently massage to combine. Cover and keep in the fridge for at least 1 hour or overnight.

5   Serve on a bagel or toast, spread with a layer of cream cheese. Top with carrot lox, pickled red onion and capers, then sprinkle with chopped chives.

Tip Remember to allow least 1 hour for the carrot to marinate.

 4   15 mins   10–12 mins   Up to 7 days

Roasted Parsnip and Celeriac with Garlicky Grains and Creamy Tahini Sauce

Served on a big platter in the middle of the table, hearty root vegetables bring comfort to dark winter days. Roasting the veg enhances their sweet, earthy flavours, with cumin and a subtle bittersweet sharpness and liquorice taste from the caraway seeds. Served on garlicky grains, it's all brought together by a creamy tahini sauce.

1kg combination of parsnips
   and celeriac
4 tbsp olive oil
1 tsp ground cumin
1 tsp caraway seeds
1 bulb of garlic
250g barley, freekeh or brown rice
2 small bunches of fresh herbs
   (I used parsley and tarragon)
zest and juice of 2 lemons
2 tbsp tahini
1 tsp wholegrain mustard
pinch of sugar (optional)
salt and black pepper
sesame seeds, to garnish

1 Heat the oven to 200°C/180°C fan/gas 6.

2 Slice the parsnips in half lengthways and the celeriac into roughly 3–4cm chunks. Place them in a roasting tin and toss with 2 tablespoons of the olive oil, the cumin and caraway seeds. Snuggle the whole garlic bulb into the edge of the tin and roast for 35–40 minutes.

3 Meanwhile, cook your grains according to the packet instructions, then drain and tip into a bowl. Roughly chop the herbs and add most to the bowl, reserving some for a garnish. Add the zest and juice of 1 lemon, along with the remaining olive oil. Season with salt and pepper and toss well.

4 Mix the tahini with the mustard and the zest and juice of half a lemon. Adding 1 tablespoon of water at a time, mix until it has a drizzleable consistency. Season well with salt and pepper. Taste and add a pinch of sugar if it feels a little sharp.

5 Once the veg is cooked, take the garlic and squeeze it into the grains; it should be soft and golden. Mix well, then tip the garlicky grains onto a platter. Top with the roasted parsnips and celeriac. Drizzle with the zesty tahini sauce, scatter with the sesame seeds and remaining herbs and serve with the zest and juice of the remaining half lemon.

Tip Play around with different veg, such as fennel, carrot, sweet potato, swede and beetroot.

 4–8   10 mins   35–40 mins   Up to 7 days   Up to 1 month

Loaded Nachos and Carrot Cheese Sauce

Nachos are the ideal party dish to bring everyone to the table. You can swap in chickpeas or kidney beans and play around with the other toppings, but the hero of the dish is the creamy, cheesy, velvety sauce. It's great poured over roasted cauliflower or baked potatoes too. *Photo overleaf*

1–2 large packs of tortilla chips
1 x 400g tin black beans, drained and rinsed
¼ red cabbage, thinly shredded
½ x quantity Killer Tofu 'Ground Beef' (page 128)

Carrot nacho cheese
150g carrots, not peeled and roughly chopped
100g new potatoes, not peeled and roughly chopped
2 garlic cloves
1 tbsp tomato purée
2 tsp cornflour
65ml milk (I use oat)
juice of ½ lemon
3 tbsp nutritional yeast
1 tsp chilli powder
½ tsp ground turmeric
pinch of salt
¼ tsp black pepper

Sour cream
120g raw cashews, soaked in hot water for 20–30 minutes, or overnight
2 tbsp apple cider vinegar
juice of ½ lemon
100ml cold water
pinch of salt

To serve (your choice)
halved cherry tomatoes, shredded lettuce, sliced red chillies, Pickled Red Onion (page 267), black olives, roughly chopped fresh coriander, lime wedges, guacamole, salsa

1 To make the carrot nacho cheese: bring a pan of salted water to the boil, add the carrots and potato and cook for about 10 minutes, until soft. Drain well, then transfer the veg to a high-speed blender. Add all the remaining ingredients and blend until very smooth. Set aside.

2 To make the vegan sour cream: drain the soaked cashews and rinse in cold water. Add all the ingredients to a high-speed blender and blend until very smooth. Set aside.

3 Preheat the oven to 180°C/160°C fan/gas 4.

4 In a large baking tin, add a layer of tortilla chips, black beans, red cabbage and a drizzle of the nacho cheese. Add a second layer of tortilla chips with my killer tofu 'ground beef' and another drizzle of nacho cheese, then bake for 8–10 minutes, until lightly crispy and golden brown.

5 Remove the nachos from the oven and top with the sour cream, plus your choice of cherry tomatoes, shredded lettuce, sliced chillies, pickled red onion, black olives and fresh coriander. Serve hot, with lime wedges to squeeze over, and guacamole and salsa on the side.

Tips Most tortilla chips are made from corn, which is naturally gluten free, but if gluten is an issue for you, check the label.

When making the Killer Tofu 'Ground Beef', use tamari, a version of soy sauce made without wheat.

The nachos will serve 2 as a main meal or 6 as a side or sharing dish.

If you want to make the vegan sour cream, put the cashews to soak before you start to cook – or even the night before.

The carrot nacho cheese will keep in the fridge for 3–5 days, or in the freezer for 1 month.

   2–6   10 mins   20 mins   **GF**

Root Vegetables

Creamy Leek and Parsnip Soup with Parsnip Peel Crisps

Leeks and parsnips go hand in hand in this sweet and earthy soup, with a flash of fire from ginger and turmeric, lifted by fresh lemon and finished with Carrot Top Pesto. Bringing all the drama and impact to your table, a tower of baked parsnip crisps transforms a simple bowl of soup into something spectacular!

6 parsnips, 5 not peeled and cut into
   1.5cm pieces, reserve 1 for garnish
2 tbsp extra-virgin olive oil
2 large leeks, including tops,
   cut into 1.5cm pieces
1½ tsp salt
1 tsp black pepper
1 bay leaf
1 tsp ground turmeric
4 garlic cloves, minced
1 tbsp fresh ginger, grated
1 shallot, diced
950ml veg stock or water
zest and juice of 1 lemon

To serve
4 tsp olive oil
4 tbsp crème fraîche
4 tbsp Carrot Top Pesto (page 28)

1   Preheat the oven to 180°C/160°C fan/gas 4.

2   With a vegetable or Y peeler, peel 1 parsnip into long thin ribbons. Place the peelings on a lined baking tray and bake in the oven for about 7 minutes, until crispy and golden; keep an eye on them so they don't burn. Set aside while you make the soup.

3   Heat the oil in a large saucepan or Dutch oven over medium heat. Add the leeks, 5 remaining parsnips, salt and black pepper, and cook, stirring occasionally, for 8–10 minutes.

4   Add the bay leaf, turmeric, garlic, ginger and shallot, and cook for 3–5 minutes until the veg is soft and fragrant. Increase the heat to high, pour in the stock and bring to the boil. Reduce the heat and simmer for 8–10 minutes.

5   Remove the bay leaf, and then use an immersion blender to purée the veg with the lemon zest and juice until it has a creamy consistency. If you like a thinner consistency, add a little extra stock or water and purée again.

6   Remove from the heat and serve the soup with the parsnip peel crisps, a drizzle of olive oil, the crème fraîche and carrot top pesto.

 4
 10 mins
 30–35 mins
 Up to 3 days
 Up to 1 month
GF

Midweek Carrot and Potato Tray Bake

Weeknight cooking doesn't get much easier than a tray bake. You whack everything in a roasting tin and then let the oven do the job for you! This colourful dish is great served in the middle of the table if you have friends over too. Don't skip the herby yoghurt sauce: it's bright, fresh and cooling, balancing the earthy, smoky, spicy flavours of the veg.

600g carrots, not peeled
1kg potatoes, not peeled (I use a mix
   of sweet potatoes and new potatoes)
2 red onions, cut into chunky wedges
1 garlic bulb
2 tbsp olive oil
350g sausages
6–8 tbsp tagine paste
handful of fresh parsley,
   roughly chopped
50g almonds, toasted and
   roughly chopped
salt and black pepper

Minty yoghurt
zest and juice of 1 lime
3 tbsp fresh mint leaves
120g yoghurt
pinch of salt

1   Preheat the oven to 200°C/180°C fan/gas 6.

2   Give the carrots a quick wash and roughly chop into batons. Roughly chop the potatoes into wedges and quarter the new potatoes; the key is to keep the veg at similar sizes so they cook evenly.

3   Arrange in a large roasting tray with the onion wedges. Snuggle in the garlic bulb, drizzle with olive oil, season with salt and black pepper and roast for 15–20 minutes.

4   Add the sausages to the tray, along with the tagine paste, toss well and roast for 15–20 minutes, until the carrots and potatoes are crisp and the sausages are browned.

5   Meanwhile, in a food processor or blender, blitz all the minty yoghurt ingredients until smooth and vibrant.

6   Squeeze the flesh from the garlic bulb into the tray and give everything a final toss. Drizzle with most of the minty yoghurt and finish with the parsley and toasted almonds. Serve straight from the pan, with the remaining minty yoghurt for people to add at the table.

Tips Try it with different spice pastes - any kind of curry paste or even Thai green curry. Or get creative make your own!

Try subbing carrot for celeriac.

If storing leftovers in the freezer, be sure to allow them to come to room temperature before heating up in the oven.

 4–8   15 mins   30–40 mins   Up to 7 days   Up to 1 month   GF

Carrot and Beetroot with Tahini Balsamic Vinaigrette

This colourful salad goes with everything from burgers or slow-roasted veg to my Nut Roast Cake with All the Trimmings (page 70), Grilled Courgette and Miso-Almond 'Ricotta' Involtini (page 121) or Zesty and Herby Summer Orzo Salad (page 52). Stunning as a side dish on a festive table or perfect for a mid-week lunch.

50g pistachios
2 tbsp extra-virgin olive oil
2 tsp balsamic vinegar
1 tbsp tahini
zest and juice of 1 lemon
1 tsp Dijon mustard
5 carrots, peeled lengthways
   into ribbons
3 small beetroot (any colour),
   thinly sliced on a mandoline
2 tbsp freshly chopped mint
salt and black pepper

1 In a small frying pan over medium heat, toast the pistachios until lightly brown, shaking the pan occasionally – this should take 3–5 minutes. Leave to cool and then chop roughly. Set aside.

2 Whisk together the olive oil, balsamic vinegar, tahini, lemon juice and mustard until smooth and creamy. Set aside.

3 Place the carrots and beetroot in a large bowl. Pour over half the dressing and toss to coat; season to taste with salt and pepper. Leave for 6–8 minutes so the beetroot softens up a little bit.

4 Transfer the carrots and beetroot to a large serving plate or bowl and spoon over the rest of the dressing. Scatter over the lemon zest, chopped mint and pistachios.

Tip Want more bulk?
Add crumbled feta.

 4–8   15 mins   5 mins   Up to 3 days

Root Vegetables

Carrot Top Pesto

I have to be honest: I used to throw away my carrot tops all the time, mainly because I didn't know what to do with them, and they took up too much space in the fridge. I've since turned over a new leaf. Make sure that you wash the tops thoroughly to remove any earth. You'll be left with a beautiful green bouquet that makes a deliciously earthy pesto. This fan favourite is great for pasta and pizzas.

green tops from a large bunch
  of carrots, rinsed
1 bunch of fresh basil, including stems
3 tbsp sunflower or pumpkin seeds
20g raw cashews or almonds
2 garlic cloves
5 tbsp nutritional yeast
2 tbsp cold water
5 tbsp extra-virgin olive oil

1 Put the carrot tops, basil, seeds, nuts, garlic, nutritional yeast and water into a food processor.

2 Begin to blend at a low speed, then slowly stream in the olive oil as you increase the speed, until mostly smooth.

Tip Pesto can be made 1 day ahead. Store in a clean jar or container, and pour in a 1cm layer of olive oil to prevent browning. Keep in the fridge.

 8 +

 5 mins

 Up to 2 weeks

 Up to 1 month

GF

Root Vegetables

Quick Pickled Carrots

Ready in minutes, these super-speedy pickled carrots add instant crunch, acidity and an amazing flash of colour to brighten any dish. Try them on rice dishes, in stir-fries, on top of the Loaded Nachos on page 19, in a crispy tofu sandwich or in the tacos on page 142.

475g carrots, sliced diagonally, 5mm thick, or grated
1 tbsp black peppercorns
1 tbsp black or brown mustard seeds
1 tsp coriander seeds
175ml white wine vinegar or apple cider vinegar
50ml water
3 tbsp sugar
2 tsp salt

1 Put the carrots into a large sterilised preserving jar. Add the peppercorns, mustard seeds and coriander seeds and set aside.

2 Put the vinegar, water, sugar and salt in a pan over medium heat and simmer, stirring, until the sugar and salt are fully dissolved.

3 Pour the warm brine over the carrots, ensuring that the carrots are fully submerged. If needed, add more vinegar or water to cover them.

4 Securely seal the jar, then shake to combine. Chill for at least 30 minutes to 1 hour before serving. For optimal flavour, marinate overnight or for up to 24 hours.

Tips For a spicier flavour, add 1 tsp chilli flakes and 2 garlic cloves, thinly sliced or crushed.

Keep in a sealed jar in the fridge for up to 2 weeks.

You can sub the carrots for beetroot. They will have an incredible colour!

 8 + 15 mins 10 mins Up to 2 weeks GF

Beetroot Bucatini

Be amazed at how the beetroot turns the pasta a majestic ruby red in this creamy, vibrant dish. It's enough to convince anyone that beetroot is incredible. Add the sauce to anything from salads to pizza to pasta. This is one of my favourite dishes in this book!

380g bucatini, spaghetti or linguine
40g feta, crumbled, to serve

Beetroot sauce
1 large beetroot, including the stems and leaves
1 tbsp olive oil
1 onion, chopped
2 garlic cloves, finely chopped or crushed
1 tbsp chopped parsley stems
1 tbsp chopped fresh basil stems, plus basil leaves to garnish
4 tbsp nutritional yeast
juice of ½ lemon
1 tsp salt
½ tsp black pepper
70ml oat milk

Crispy garlic breadcrumbs
1 tbsp olive oil
1 garlic clove, grated or thinly sliced
50g breadcrumbs (home-made from a stale loaf, or shop-bought)

Tips Use gluten-free pasta and breadcrumbs if you prefer.

Store any leftover pasta and garlic breadcrumbs separately.

1 To make the beetroot sauce: bring a pan of water to the boil, add the whole beetroot and cook for 10–15 minutes or until tender. Drain the beetroot and set aside to cool for a few minutes, then cut into quarters.

2 Meanwhile, in a non-stick frying pan over medium heat, heat the olive oil and cook the onion, garlic, parsley and basil stems for 3–5 minutes until fragrant and soft. Remove from the heat; do not wash the pan.

3 Put the beetroot into a food processor or blender, add the onion mixture, nutritional yeast, lemon juice, salt and pepper. Pulse for 1 minute, then, with the motor running, stream in the milk. Blend on high speed until very smooth. If the sauce is too thick, add a little more milk, 1 tablespoon at a time, to loosen.

4 Bring a large pan of salted water to the boil, add the bucatini and cook for 9 minutes or until al dente. Drain the pasta, reserving 4–5 tablespoons of the pasta cooking water.

5 Meanwhile, prepare the crispy garlic breadcrumbs. In a separate frying pan, heat the oil over medium heat, add the garlic and fry for 1 minute until lightly browned. Add the breadcrumbs and cook, stirring frequently, until the breadcrumbs are lightly charred and fragrant, about 2–3 minutes. Remove from the heat and set aside.

6 In the same frying pan used for the onion and garlic, add the cooked pasta and beetroot sauce and stir well over low–medium heat for 2 minutes. If too thick, stir in some of the reserved pasta water.

7 Serve the pasta in bowls or on plates, garnished with roughly torn basil leaves, crumbled feta cheese and crispy garlic breadcrumbs.

 4   15 mins   25–35 mins   1–2 days   Up to 1 month

Root Vegetables

Marinated Beetroot with Toasted Pistachios, Orange and Mint

Baked until tender, the beetroot is then marinated with shallot and ginger. Orange segments, cinnamon, toasted pistachios and fresh mint are added just before serving on creamy yoghurt to make a complex, sweet autumnal salad.

450g small yellow or red beetroot
120ml sherry vinegar or rice vinegar
4 tbsp olive oil
60ml water
1 shallot, finely chopped
1 tbsp grated fresh ginger
1 orange, zested, then segmented
¼ tsp ground cinnamon
40g raw pistachios, toasted
  and chopped
2 tbsp freshly chopped mint
220g thick yoghurt (I use
  oat or coconut)
salt and black pepper

1 Preheat the oven to 200°C/180°C fan/gas 6.

2 Put the beetroot in a baking dish. In a small bowl mix together 60ml of the vinegar, 2 tablespoons of the olive oil, the water and salt and pepper. Pour over the beetroot and toss until well coated. Cover with foil and bake for about 40 minutes, until soft and tender. Remove from the oven and leave to cool for 5–10 minutes, then cut into quarters while still warm.

3 Meanwhile, in a large bowl, mix the shallot and ginger with the remaining vinegar and olive oil, and season with a pinch of salt. Add the warm beetroot quarters, toss to coat and leave in the fridge to marinate for at least 45 minutes and up to 3 days.

4 To serve, add the orange segments, cinnamon, most of the pistachios and mint to the beetroot and, and gently combine.

5 Spread the yoghurt over the base of a serving plate, top with the marinated beetroot and sprinkle over the orange zest and the remaining pistachios and mint.

Tips Marinate the beetroot up to 2-3 days ahead, cover and chill.

If you buy beetroot with their green tops, you can chop the greens and cook them like spinach, or sub the carrot tops for beetroot leaves in the Carrot Top Pesto on page 28.

 6   15 mins   40 mins   Up to 3 days   GF

The Best Roast Potatoes

Since living in the UK, I've realised I've been cooking roast potatoes wrong my entire life! As all Brits know, the secret is to boil the potatoes for a few minutes first, then rough up the outsides before cooking them in the oven in already-hot oil. This three-stage process will guarantee you perfect roasties every time!

1.8kg large potatoes, not peeled,
  cut into 5cm pieces
100ml olive oil
2 tbsp vegetable oil
30g butter
6 garlic cloves, crushed
4 long fresh rosemary sprigs
6 fresh thyme sprigs
salt

1 Preheat the oven to 220°C/200°C fan/gas 7.

2 Put the potatoes in a large pan of salted water. Bring to the boil over medium–high heat, then reduce to a simmer and cook for about 5 minutes, until the potatoes are fork-tender on the outside but still firm in the middle.

3 When the potatoes are nearly ready, add the oils and butter to a large roasting tin, mix together then place in the hot oven for at least 5 minutes until the oils and butter are hot.

4 Drain the potatoes well then return them to their pan, uncovered, to steam-dry for about 2 minutes. Holding the lid on securely with both hands, give the pan a good shake, just enough to fluff up the outer edges of the potatoes; don't shake the pan too hard or the potatoes will break apart.

5 Take the roasting tin out of the oven and carefully coat the potatoes in the hot oils. Spread out the potatoes to keep them separate in the roasting tin as this will ensure each one gets super-crispy in the oven. Roast the potatoes for 20 minutes, turning them halfway through. If they are browning too quickly, reduce the heat.

6 Add the garlic, rosemary and thyme sprigs, turn the potatoes again then return to the oven for a further 10 minutes, until the potatoes are golden brown and the skin is deliciously crispy. Transfer the potatoes, garlic, thyme and rosemary to a serving plate using a slotted spoon or tongs to drain off any excess oil.

Tip These roasties are great as a side dish with my Roast Dinner Tart (page 199) and Nut Roast Cake on page 70.

 8   5 mins   35–40 mins   Up to 7 days   **GF**

Potato and Spring Onion Potato Cakes

If you have some potatoes languishing in a drawer, use them in these potato cakes today! Just pull off any shoots, but if the potatoes have turned green, it's best to compost them. With the crunchy Asian-style slaw, this is a great brunch or light lunch, or make mini versions to serve as canapés.

1kg potatoes
splash of milk
2 tbsp self-raising flour, plus more
   for dusting
2 tsp grated fresh ginger
1 bunch spring onions, finely sliced
½ small bunch of fresh coriander,
   roughly chopped
3 tbsp olive oil
salt and black pepper
coconut yoghurt, to serve

Hispi slaw
1 hispi cabbage, shredded
½ small bunch of fresh coriander,
   roughly chopped, plus more
   to garnish
2 tbsp sesame seeds
zest and juice of 2 limes
1 tbsp sesame oil
1 tsp sugar

1   Cut the potatoes into large chunks, cover with cold salted water, place over a high heat and bring to the boil. Cook for about 15 minutes, until very soft. Drain well in a colander and allow to steam-dry for 3–5 minutes.

2   Meanwhile, mix all ingredients for the slaw together in a large bowl, season with a generous pinch of salt and set aside.

3   Mash the potatoes and milk in a large bowl; it's fine if there are a few chunks of potatoes. Season with salt and pepper. Add the flour, ginger, spring onions and coriander and set aside. Preheat the oven to 120°C/100°C fan/gas ½.

4   Roll the potato mixture into 12 even balls, then dust with flour. Heat the olive oil in a large frying pan. Add the mashed potato balls, 4 at a time, and using the back of a spatula, press down to flatten them. Fry for 5–7 minutes on each side until golden brown and crispy.

5   Set the pancakes aside on a lined baking tray and slide into the oven to keep warm while you cook the rest. Keep an eye on the cooked pancakes so they don't overcook and dry out; reduce the heat if needed.

6   Serve the potato cakes garnished with coriander leaves and topped with a dollop of the yoghurt, with the slaw on the side.

Tips If you have leftover mashed potatoes, give it new life in these potato cakes.

You can use any potatoes – sweet potatoes are great, or even celeriac.

 12 cakes   10 mins   1 hour   Up to 3 days   Up to 1 month

Crispy Smashed Potatoes with Spicy Lemon Mayo

This is a BIG fan favourite. Brushing the potatoes with tomato purée before roasting them gives them an amazing rich colour and a surprise extra layer of flavour. I love to serve these as part of a savoury brunch fry-up, with scrambled tofu, baked mushrooms and roasted tomatoes. But they also make a fantastic starter or side dish.

20 new potatoes, not peeled
1 tbsp extra-virgin olive oil
1 tbsp tomato purée
zest and juice of ½ lemon
generous pinch of salt
¼ tsp black pepper
4 tbsp mayo
1 tsp smoked paprika
¼ tsp chilli powder

To serve
Pickled Red Onion (page 267)
2 tbsp roughly chopped fresh dill
2 tbsp roughly chopped fresh chives

1 Preheat the oven to 200°C/180°C fan/gas 6.

2 Bring a large pan of salted water to the boil, add the potatoes and cook for 10–15 minutes, until they are just soft enough that you can poke a fork into them, then drain.

3 Meanwhile, whisk the olive oil, tomato purée, lemon zest, salt and pepper until smooth.

4 Gently press the potatoes with the base of an empty jam jar until the skin breaks, then place them on a large baking sheet. Brush each potato with the oil and tomato mixture and bake for 20 minutes or until golden and the edges are crispy, rotating the baking sheet after about 10 minutes.

5 To a small bowl or jar, add the mayo, smoked paprika, chilli powder and lemon juice and stir or shake for a few seconds until smooth and combined.

6 Put the crispy potatoes on a serving platter and top with a few dollops of the spicy lemon mayo, some pickled red onion and fresh herbs.

Tips Smaller potatoes are best.

For a main meal you may like to add some grated cheese after baking or serve with some steamed peas.

If you have any leftover potatoes*, keep them in the fridge and reheat until crispy.

  2–4   15 mins   30–35 mins   1–2 days* ❄ Up to 3 months (Just potatoes)

Soft and Fluffy Potato Rolls

Whether you're cooking these rolls from scratch or using leftover mashed or baked potatoes, you're in luck: they're better than any rolls you can buy! You don't need to be an expert baker to make these gorgeous fluffy rolls as the dough is very forgiving, even if you over- or under-knead it. As with any yeast dough, you'll need to allow 1½–2 hours for the dough to rise – but you're free to get on with other things in that time. These fan favourites have a buttery, salty top and a super-soft centre – perfect for sandwiches or use them for my Super 'Meatball' Sliders (page 68).

300ml warm water
2¼ tsp dried active yeast
1 tsp sugar
625g plain flour or gluten-free flour, plus more for dusting
2 tsp salt
90g butter, at room temperature
270g cooked potatoes, mashed, skins on
vegetable oil, for greasing
flaky sea salt, for sprinkling

1 In a small bowl, whisk together the warm water, yeast and sugar for about 1 minute, until the sugar has dissolved and the mixture is foamy. Set aside for about 5 minutes.

2 Mix the flour and salt in a large mixing bowl, then add the yeast mixture, 60g of butter and the mashed potatoes. Using your hands or a mixer fitted with a dough hook, knead well until all the ingredients are incorporated and the dough begins to feel smooth. Shape into a ball, drizzle a little oil around the inside of the bowl so the dough doesn't stick to it, cover with a clean tea towel and leave for about 1 hour, or until doubled in size.

3 Grease a 33 x 23cm baking tin with oil. Dust the worktop with flour. Punch the dough to deflate, then tip it onto the worktop and divide and roll into 12 equal balls. Place the balls in the greased baking tin and leave to prove for 30–45 minutes.

4 Preheat the oven to 200°C/180°C fan/gas 6.

5 Melt the remaining butter and brush it over the top of each dough ball. Sprinkle with flaky sea salt and bake for 25 minutes until the tops are golden brown and the dough is cooked. Test by tapping the underside of a roll: it should sound hollow. Transfer to a wire rack to cool slightly before serving.

Tips If you prefer, use gluten-free flour.

Swap potato for sweet potato.

Mash the potatoes until smooth or leave a few lumps – it's your call.

Keep leftovers, but not in the fridge, for up to 5 days.

 12 rolls 20 mins 25 mins Up to 1 month **GF**

Root Vegetables

Spiced Potato Pancakes

This recipe is inspired by dosas: thin pancakes originating in South India, made from a fermented batter and curled into a dome and often filled with spicy potatoes. I was motivated to make this recipe because potatoes are one of the most-wasted foods around the world. In the UK alone, over 4 million of them are wasted every day – that could make a lot of pancakes! The recipe is super-quick and easy to make, although making the pancakes requires a bit of practice. Follow along below, then fill your pancake with spiced potatoes and serve with an Indian chutney.

Spiced potatoes
300g baby potatoes, not peeled,
  cut in half
2 tbsp butter
2 tbsp milk
2 tbsp olive oil
1 onion, finely chopped
1 tbsp grated fresh ginger
1 tsp black mustard seeds
1 tsp coriander seeds
2 tsp garam masala
½ tsp ground turmeric
4 curry leaves
100g spinach or chopped kale
salt and black pepper

Pancakes
80g gram flour
80g buckwheat flour
1½ tsp bicarbonate of soda
pinch of salt

To serve
chutney of your choice,
  (I've served them with
  mango chutney)
thick yoghurt

1   Bring a pan of salted water to the boil, add the potatoes and cook for 10–15 minutes, until soft. Drain off all the water and let the potatoes sit in the pan, uncovered, for a few minutes. In a bowl, lightly mash the potatoes with the butter and the milk until slightly chunky; season with salt and pepper. Set aside.

2   In a large frying pan, heat the oil over medium heat and fry the onion and ginger for 7–8 minutes, until soft and fragrant. Add the mustard seeds and coriander seeds and let them cook for a few minutes until they pop, then add the garam masala, turmeric and curry leaves and cook, stirring, for 1 minute.

3   Lower the heat and add the mashed potatoes to the onion mixture, then stir in the spinach or kale until wilted. Splash in a little water if the potatoes stick to the pan. Set aside.

4   To make the pancakes, mix all the ingredients in a bowl, adding enough water to make a pourable, runny batter. Heat a non-stick flat griddle or a large non-stick frying pan over medium–high heat. Pour about half a ladleful of the batter onto the centre of the griddle, then quickly and confidently spread the batter around the griddle, using the bottom of the ladle in a circular motion. The pancake should be fairly thin, and dry on the top. Cook, without flipping, for about 1–2 minutes, until golden brown and the edges are crispy and beginning to curl. Remove from the griddle and cook three more pancakes in the same way.

5   Serve the spiced potatoes with the pancakes, the chutney and yoghurt.

 4
 10 mins
 25–30 mins
 1–3 days*
 Up to 1 month
 GF

Tips *Keep spiced potatoes
in the fridge for 1-3 days. You
can make them in advance,
but make the pancakes
just before you are ready to eat.

Gram flour is made from ground
chickpeas and is gluten-free.
Buckwheat flour is naturally gluten-
free, but brands vary: if gluten
is an issue for you, check the label.

Roasted Sweet Potatoes with Creamy and Zesty Tahini Peanut Butter

Comfort food at its finest. Slather the rich, tangy tahini butter onto these mouth-watering roasted sweet potatoes and you have a perfect pairing. This recipe is easy to make, utterly delicious and always a hit. Serve as a side dish or with a big salad.

3 large sweet potatoes (any colour), halved lengthways
1 tbsp olive oil
1 tbsp toasted white or black sesame seeds or a mix
flaky sea salt and black pepper
lime wedges, to serve

Creamy and zesty tahini peanut butter
2 tbsp tahini
1 tbsp peanut butter, smooth or crunchy
5 tbsp unsalted butter, at room temperature
zest and juice of 1 lime
1 tbsp soy sauce or tamari
2 tsp toasted sesame oil

1   Preheat the oven to 200°C/180°C fan/gas 6. Line a baking sheet with baking parchment.

2   Place the halved sweet potatoes on the baking sheet and drizzle with the olive oil. Roast for 15–20 minutes, or until lightly charred around the edges and soft in the middle.

3   Meanwhile, make the creamy and zesty tahini peanut butter: in a bowl combine the tahini, peanut butter, butter, lime juice and zest, soy sauce and sesame oil, and mix together well.

4   Transfer the cooked sweet potatoes to a serving plate and spread the tahini peanut butter over the top of each potato half. Season with sea salt and black pepper, scatter with toasted sesame seeds and serve with lime wedges.

Tips If gluten is an issue for you, ensure you use tamari, a version of soy sauce made without wheat.

For more crunch, dice the sweet potatoes before roasting.

For an elevated sauce, stir a tablespoon of miso into the tahini peanut butter.

Make extra tahini butter and add it to your favourite roasted veg or rice bowls.

 8
 5 mins
 15–20 mins
 Up to 3 days
 Up to 1 month
GF

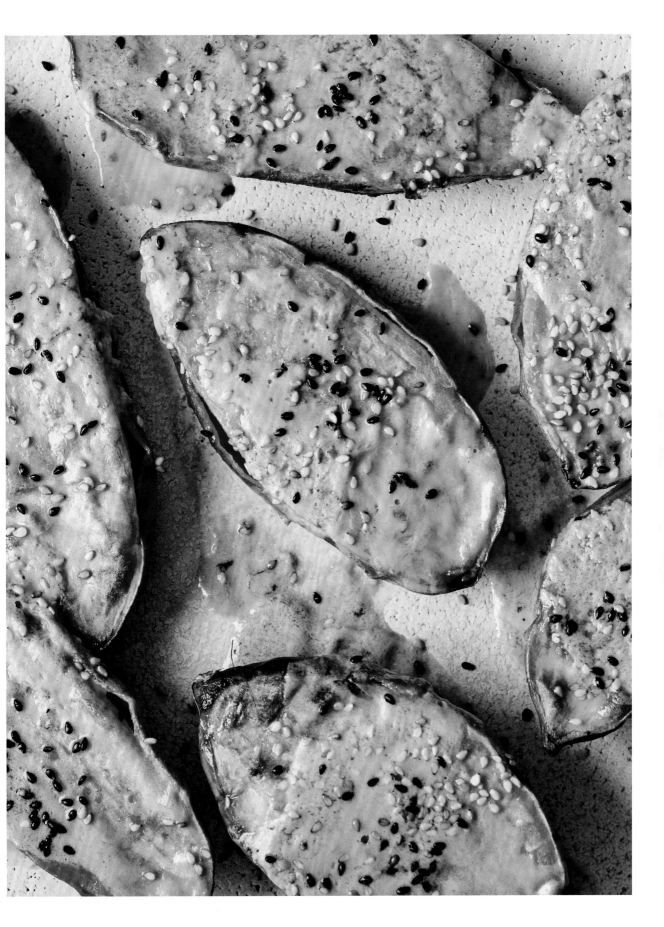

Carrot Pecan Cake and Orange Drizzle

I'm often asked to share carrot recipes, especially carrot cake recipes. I guess people like carrot cake. I aim to please, so here's a super-moist cake with a sweet, citrusy drizzle, making this my best carrot cake yet.

butter, for greasing
340g plain flour
2 tsp baking powder
1 tsp bicarbonate of soda
1 tsp salt
1 tsp ground cinnamon
1 tsp ground ginger
1 tsp ground cardamom
¼ tsp ground nutmeg
55g pecans, crushed

Wet ingredients
250ml soy milk
120g apple sauce
75g light brown sugar
zest of 1 orange, reserving the juice
   for the drizzle
4½ tbsp maple syrup
4 tbsp vegetable oil
150g carrot, finely grated

Orange drizzle
150g icing sugar
2 tbsp orange juice

1   Preheat the oven to 180°C/160°C fan/gas 4. Butter a 24cm bundt tin.

2   Sift all the dry ingredients, apart from the pecans, into a large mixing bowl.

3   In another bowl, whisk together the soy milk, apple sauce, light brown sugar, orange zest, maple syrup and oil.

4   Make a well in the middle of the flour mixture and pour in the milk mixture. Using a rubber spatula or wooden spoon, gently fold together, until no streaks of flour remain. Add the grated carrot and pecans to the bowl and gently fold through.

5   Carefully pour the batter into the prepared bundt tin. Smooth the top, using the back of a spoon. Bake the cake for 30–32 minutes, or until it is cooked all the way through: a skewer inserted into the cake should come out clean.

6   Place the cake – still in its tin – on a wire rack and leave to cool for 10 minutes. Place a cutting board on the exposed side of the cake and carefully and confidently flip it over then gently remove the bundt tin. Place the cake back on the wire rack to cool completely.

7   For the orange drizzle, mix the icing sugar and half the orange juice in a bowl, adding more orange juice to get your preferred consistency. Drizzle the orange glaze over the cake.

Tip Store in an airtight container at room temperature for up to 3 days, or (without the drizzle) in the fridge for up to 7 days.

 8   20 mins   30 mins   7 days   Up to 1 month

2– Grains

Rice
Mixed Grains
Pasta
Bread

Roasted Fennel and Quinoa Salad with Apple and Tahini

My niece is a little over two years old and she loves talking with me about all things food and cooking! I made this fennel and quinoa salad for her christening, and it was a major hit! It's a great recipe to made ahead to take on picnics or pack into a lunchbox for work. To add more bulk, add some baked tofu or crispy chickpeas.

90g quinoa, soaked for 10–15 minutes, then rinsed
240ml water
1 small bulb of fennel, thinly sliced, reserving fronds to garnish
2 tbsp olive oil
1 tbsp tahini
zest and juice of ½ lemon
2 tsp Dijon mustard
1 apple, cored and cut into half-moon slices
½ cucumber, diced
2 tbsp freshly chopped dill
2 tbsp freshly chopped mint
30g toasted chopped nuts or seeds
salt and black pepper

1 Put the quinoa, water and a pinch of salt in a pan over medium heat. Bring to the boil and simmer, uncovered, until all of the liquid has been absorbed, about 10–15 minutes. Set aside to cool.

2 Meanwhile, preheat the oven to 200°C/180°C fan/gas 6. Line a baking sheet with baking parchment.

3 Toss the fennel with 1 tablespoon of the olive oil and season with salt and pepper. Spread out on the baking sheet and roast for 12–14 minutes, tossing halfway through, until the fennel is lightly charred and the edges are golden. Set aside to cool.

4 Meanwhile in a small jar or bowl, add the remaining olive oil, tahini, lemon juice, zest and mustard; close the lid and shake vigorously, or whisk until smooth.

5 Fluff the cooled quinoa with a fork into a large bowl. Add the roasted fennel, apple and cucumber, the herbs and some of the toasted nuts or seeds. Drizzle the tahini sauce over and toss until combined. Garnish with the remaining nuts or seeds and the reserved fennel fronds.

Tips Don't add the dressing until you're ready to serve.

If the roasted fennel is wet, pat dry with kitchen paper to remove excess water.

 4–8　 15 mins　 15 mins　 Up to 3 days　 Up to 1 month　**GF**

Zesty and Herby Summer Orzo Salad

Fast and friendly, this vibrant pasta salad is super-easy to make, and it's great for using up leftover fresh herbs and feta. Perfect for cooling you down on hot summer days, as a speedy midweek meal or a summer side dish for picnics.

250g orzo or any short pasta or grain
120g frozen peas
1 tbsp extra-virgin olive oil
zest and juice of 1 lemon
3 baby cucumbers, diced
2 tbsp freshly chopped mint
2 tbsp freshly chopped dill
2 tbsp freshly chopped parsley
30g feta, crumbled
generous pinch of salt
¼ tsp black pepper
lemon wedges, to serve

1 Bring a large pan of salted water to the boil, add the orzo and cook for 8–10 minutes, or until al dente. Drain, run under cold water and drain well, then transfer to a large serving bowl.

2 Meanwhile, put the frozen peas in a bowl and cover with freshly boiled water; leave for 1–2 minutes until bright green. Drain and run the peas under cold water for 30–45 seconds. Drain again and set aside.

3 Drizzle the olive oil, lemon juice and zest over the cooked orzo. Add all the remaining ingredients and toss until well combined. Chill until ready to serve. Serve on a large plate, with lemon wedges.

Tip Use gluten-free pasta if you prefer.

 4–8   5 mins   15 mins Up to 5 days

Crunchy Butter Rice, Cherries and Toasted Hazelnuts

This is my take on a tahdig - an incredible Persian crispy rice dish. Jewelled with sweet and tart dried cherries, hazelnuts, onions, peppers and fresh thyme, it's a real showstopper of a meal. Flip it over in front of your guests to reveal the delicious crunchy rice on top. You are going to have to fight the urge to stir the rice when it's cooking - trust the process!

310g basmati rice
6 tbsp butter
1 tbsp olive oil
1 onion, finely chopped
1 red pepper, seeded, thinly sliced
65g dried cherries, raisins or sultanas
1 tbsp ground coriander
salt

To garnish
50g toasted hazelnuts, chopped
fresh thyme sprigs

1   Rinse and wash the rice in a large bowl of cold water. Change the water frequently until the water is clear. Bring a large pan of salted water to the boil, add the rice and boil for about 3–4 minutes, until al dente. Drain the rice in a sieve, transfer to a bowl and set aside.

2   In a non-stick frying pan, melt 2 tablespoons of the butter with the olive oil over medium heat. Add the onion and a generous pinch of salt and cook, stirring often, for 6–8 minutes, until soft and golden. Add the red pepper and cook, stirring occasionally, for 5–7 minutes, until soft and lightly charred around the edges. Transfer the onions and red pepper to the bowl of rice, add the dried cherries and coriander and toss to combine.

3   Melt 3 tablespoons of the butter in a heavy-based pan or Dutch oven over medium heat. Spread the rice mixture in the pan in an even layer and pat down lightly. Using the handle of a wooden spoon, make four or five holes in the rice and add the remaining butter, cut into small pieces, to the holes. Cook the rice, uncovered and without stirring, for 4–5 minutes.

Continued $\longrightarrow$

 4–8   15 mins   45 mins– 1 hour   1 day   Up to 1 month   **GF**

Continued →

4 Reduce the heat and cover the pan with a clean cloth and a lid; carefully fold the cloth corners up and over the lid. Cook the rice over low heat for 30–35 minutes. Check after 20–25 minutes to see if the rice smells toasty, but not burnt. Do not be tempted to stir. Remove from the heat and let it stand for 10 minutes.

5 Fluff the rice using a fork and transfer it to a serving bowl. Using a spatula, gently remove the crusty bottom and add it to the rice. Or if you feel inclined, place the top of a large plate over the pan, grab the handles of the pan while holding the plate in place, and in one confident motion FLIP it over so that the pan is on top. Remove the pan slowly for dramatic effect. Garnish with toasted hazelnuts and small sprigs of fresh thyme.

'What's in the Fridge?' Fried Rice

A surprising ingredient people often ask me what to do with are corn cobs! This summery fried rice, coated in a peanut-sesame-lime sauce is the perfect way to celebrate them – and fried rice is also the best vehicle for using up whatever you have lurking in the bottom of your fridge. Any veg will work here, and you can use tinned sweetcorn if you don't have fresh cobs.

2 large corn cobs, husked
1 tbsp vegetable oil
4 spring onions, thinly sliced
　on diagonal
1 tbsp butter
1 large carrot, not peeled, grated
150g leftover cooked rice
3 tbsp soy sauce or tamari
2 tbsp peanut butter, or any seed
　or nut butter
1 tsp toasted sesame oil
1 tsp maple syrup
zest and juice of ½ lime

To serve
1 tbsp finely snipped fresh chives
1–2 tsp toasted sesame seeds
30g toasted peanuts, crushed

1 Bring a pan of water to the boil, add the corn cobs and cook until tender, about 5 minutes. Drain and leave to cool. Cut the corn kernels off the cobs and set them aside in a bowl.

2 Heat the oil in a large non-stick frying pan over medium heat. Set aside some spring onion to garnish and add the remaining spring onions to the frying pan; cook for about 2 minutes, stirring occasionally, until soft and lightly browned. Add the corn and butter, stir, and cook for 2–3 minutes.

3 Add the carrot and rice to the pan, stir so that the rice covers the bottom of the pan, then cook undisturbed for 4–5 minutes until the rice begins to crisp.

4 Meanwhile, in a small jar or bowl, add the soy sauce, peanut butter, sesame oil, maple syrup and lime juice; close the lid and shake vigorously, or whisk until smooth.

5 Pour the sauce over the rice mixture. Stir well to coat, and cook for about 1 minute until the rice is glossy.

6 Serve hot, topped with the lime zest, reserved spring onions, chives, sesame seeds and crushed peanuts.

Tips Tamari is a gluten-free version of soy sauce.

Save the cobs to add to a veg stock (page 260).

If you like things spicy, add chilli sauce.

Double or triple all the ingredients to serve more people.

 2   10 mins   20 mins   1 day   Up to 1 month

Baked Sundried Tomato Rice with a Golden Pastry Lid

Inspired by incredible Indian feasts, this showstopper of a dish is perfect for sharing with friends and family at your next celebration. Breaking through the golden, crispy pastry reveals what's been cooking underneath, and tomatoes are the hero of this biriyani-style pie! I've used two types: fresh for texture and sweetness, and sundried for a luxurious, umami intensity. It's all cooled down by a creamy raita and crunchy cucumber salad.

300g basmati rice
60g butter, plus more for greasing
3 onions, thinly sliced
1 tbsp garam masala
3 tbsp vegetable oil or ghee
3 garlic cloves, sliced thinly
1 tbsp grated ginger
1 tbsp ground coriander
1 tsp ground turmeric
1 tsp ground cumin
6 plum tomatoes, roughly chopped
110g sundried tomatoes, sliced in half
½ small head of cauliflower, roughly
  chopped (save the leaves to use them
  in my Cauliflower Ragù on page 146)
120g yoghurt (I use coconut)
1 sheet puff pastry
2 tsp milk, for brushing (I use oat)
1 tbsp olive oil, for brushing
1 tsp nigella seeds
1 tsp cumin seeds
½ tsp brown mustard seeds
salt and black pepper

To serve
small bunch mint, roughly
  chopped raita

Tip Great for big gatherings, try serving this with my Loaded Nachos (page 19) or for a more relaxed evening, with Roasted Fennel and Quinoa Salad (page 50).

1 Rinse the rice under cold running water until the water runs clear. Tip into a saucepan, cover with 600ml cold water, bring to the boil, then reduce to a simmer. Cover and cook for 10 minutes, then remove from the heat and leave with the lid on to steam for 10 minutes.

2 Meanwhile, melt the butter in a large saucepan over a medium heat. Add the onions and a generous pinch of salt. Cook for 8–10 minutes, stirring often, until soft and translucent. Stir in the garam masala and cook for 1 minute, then set aside.

3 In a large saucepan over a medium heat, warm the oil and fry the garlic and ginger for 1–2 minutes, until fragrant. Stir in the spices and cook for 1 minute. Add the plum tomatoes and sundried tomatoes, stir until well combined, and cook for 1 minute. Stir in the cauliflower and cook for 8–10 minutes, until the cauliflower is slightly soft. Stir in the yoghurt until incorporated, season with salt and black pepper, then remove from the heat.

4 Grease a pie dish or cake tin, approx. 23 x 20cm, with a little butter. Spoon in half of the tomato mixture, then half the rice, then repeat using up the rest of the tomatoes and rice.

5 Finish with a layer of rice. Top with the jammy onions.

Continued $\rightarrow$

 6 25 mins 45–50 mins Up to 5 days Up to 1 month

Continued $\longrightarrow$

6   Unroll the pastry sheet and cut to the size of the dish with a slight overhang. Place the pastry sheet over the top of the dish and cut 3 or 4 small holes into the surface with a knife to release the steam as it cooks. In a small bowl mix together the oat milk and olive oil, and brush over the pastry. Scatter with the nigella, cumin and brown mustard seeds.

7   Bake for 25 minutes, until the pastry is golden brown and crispy. Remove from oven and allow to cool for 5 minutes before cracking open the lid at the table. Garnish with the mint and serve with raita.

Golden Split Peas with Herby Rice

A super-easy and satisfying recipe that you can dress up with amazing toppings like toasted coconut flakes, punchy Pickled Red Onion, cool yoghurt and a pop of fresh herbs. If you have the patience or self-control, leave the split peas to sit for 12 hours or overnight, to let the spices work their magic, and reheat to serve. If (like me) you don't have self-control or are too hungry, aim to let them sit for 5–10 minutes before serving.

2 tbsp vegetable oil
1 onion, finely chopped
20g fresh ginger, not peeled, finely grated
3 garlic cloves, finely grated
210g red or yellow split peas, rinsed well and drained
2 tsp ground coriander
1 tsp cumin seeds, toasted
1 tsp ground turmeric
¼ tsp ground cinnamon
950ml water or veg stock
salt and black pepper

Herby rice
2 tbsp butter
2 tbsp chopped fresh coriander stems
2 tbsp chopped fresh mint stems
200g long grain rice (white or brown)

To serve
4 tbsp coconut flakes
zest of 1 lime
yoghurt (I use coconut yoghurt)
Pickled Red Onion (page 267)
freshly chopped coriander and mint

1 Heat the oil in a large saucepan over medium heat. Cook the onion for 5–8 minutes, until soft, stirring frequently. Add the ginger and garlic, season with salt and pepper and cook, still stirring, for 30 seconds. Stir in the split peas, ground coriander, cumin seeds, turmeric and cinnamon for 30–45 seconds, until you can smell all those delicious aromatics. Pour in half the water and bring to the boil. Reduce the heat to medium–low and simmer for 10–15 minutes, until the split peas are tender. Cover and keep warm over low heat.

2 To make the herby rice, melt the butter in a small saucepan over medium heat. Add the herb stems and cook, stirring frequently, for 2–3 minutes, until lightly brown and fragrant. Add the rice and cook, stirring occasionally, for about 2 minutes, until the rice is lightly toasted. Pour in the remaining water, bring to the boil, then reduce the heat and simmer for 10–15 minutes, until the liquid has been absorbed. Remove from the heat and cover with a lid.

3 Meanwhile, in a small frying pan over medium heat, toast the coconut flakes for 2–3 minutes, stirring often, until lightly browned. Set aside.

4 Serve the herby rice topped with lime zest and the toasted coconut flakes. Spoon the golden split peas alongside, and top with yoghurt, the pickled red onion and lots of freshly chopped herbs.

Tips Cook the split peas and serve the next day – or enjoy amazing leftovers!

Serve with my Fragrant Flatbreads (page 206).

 4   10 mins   30–45 mins   1–3 days   Up to 1 month

One-pot Pantry Pasta

One of my most popular dishes and for good reason – it's a one-pot pasta dish, and you don't even need a colander to strain the pasta! It's delicious, satisfying, takes only 20 minutes and is made with ingredients you probably already have at home. Great for lunch, weeknight meals with the family, or whenever you're feeling lazy. You will be making this time and time again.

1 tbsp olive oil
2 garlic cloves, finely chopped
125g cooked lentils (tinned are fine)
30g pitted green olives, sliced
1 tbsp tomato purée
pinch of chilli flakes
1 x 400g tin chopped tomatoes
large handful of spinach
185g spaghetti, linguine, bucatini
   or any long pasta
600ml water or veg stock
large handful of fresh basil and parsley,
   torn or roughly chopped
flaky sea salt and black pepper
extra-virgin olive oil, to serve

1   Heat the oil in a large non-stick pot over medium–low heat and fry the garlic for 1–2 minutes until fragrant and lightly brown, stirring occasionally.

2   Add the lentils, olives and tomato purée, season with salt, pepper and chilli flakes and cook, stirring, for another 2–3 minutes. Add the tomatoes and spinach and cook for 3–4 minutes, stirring until the spinach is soft and the sauce begins to bubble slightly.

3   Add the pasta and carefully pour in the water, stir, then increase the heat to medium–high and simmer for 8–10 minutes, stirring occasionally, until the pasta is al dente. If you prefer a thicker sauce, let it sit for 5 minutes before serving.

4   Serve in bowls, garnished with the torn or roughly chopped herbs, a drizzle of extra-virgin olive oil and a pinch of flaky sea salt.

Tips Use gluten-free pasta if you prefer.

Double or triple all the ingredients to serve more people.

 2   5 mins   15–20 mins   Up to 3 days   Up to 1 month

Curried Couscous with Sticky Butternut and Coriander Chutney

Wonderfully spiced chickpeas and sweet and sticky roasted butternut squash are topped with a punchy herby-lime-ginger-chilli chutney. This giant couscous platter has intense flavours and textures coming at you from every direction!

1 butternut squash
2 tbsp maple syrup
3 tbsp olive oil
1 tbsp cumin seeds
250g giant couscous
1 large onion, finely diced
2 tsp grated fresh ginger
2 garlic cloves, thinly sliced
2 tbsp curry powder
1 tbsp ground coriander
zest and juice of 1 lime
1 x 400g tin chickpeas, drained
  (save the liquid for meringues,
  see page 228)
salt and black pepper

To serve
4 tbsp yoghurt
6 tbsp toasted cashews, roughly chopped

The chutney
large handful of fresh coriander
large handful of fresh mint
zest and juice of 2 limes
1 tsp grated fresh ginger
6–8 curry leaves (optional)
3 spring onions, roughly chopped
1–2 green chillies, depending on how
  much heat you like (remove the seeds
  if you like it less hot)

Tips Giant couscous has an amazing texture but go ahead and swap it out for any grain you need to use up.

Pumpkin and celeriac will work well instead of the butternut.

1 Preheat the oven to 200°C/180°C fan/gas 6.

2 Cut the squash into half-moons, remove the seeds and set aside (you can rinse them and then toast them as a snack). Place the squash on a baking sheet. In a small bowl, mix together the maple syrup and 1 tablespoon of the oil. Drizzle over the squash and scatter with the cumin seeds. Season with salt and roast for 20 minutes, until soft and sticky. Turn on the grill and grill for 5–10 minutes further, until the squash is a little charred.

3 Bring a saucepan of salted water to the boil, and cook the giant couscous according to packet instructions. Drain well and set aside.

4 Meanwhile, heat the remaining oil in a large frying pan over a medium heat. Fry the onion and ginger with a generous pinch of salt and cook for about 5 minutes, until softened. Add the garlic, curry powder and coriander, and cook for a minute further, stirring often. Remove from the heat, add the zest and juice of the lime, then tip in the chickpeas and giant couscous and toss well. Season, to taste, with salt and black pepper.

5 To make the chutney, blitz all the ingredients in a food processor until smooth.

6 To serve, pile the curried couscous onto a platter or into bowls and top with the sticky roasted squash. Drizzle with a little yoghurt, then a little of the chutney. Scatter with toasted cashews and serve.

 4–6   20 mins   25–30 mins   Up to 5 days   Up to 1 month

Roasted Root Veg Sub Rolls

I come from Connecticut, a state in America that is known for its BIG sandwiches. My dad also owned a series of sandwich shops, so I grew up surrounded by sandwiches! In this packed-out sub – which has become my ultimate go-to sandwich – mixed root veg and cream cheese are drizzled with an intensely herby, tangy sauce. There's no pausing when you eat this sandwich, you'll just keep going in for more.

1kg mixed root veg (I used carrots, parsnips, beetroot and celeriac)
2 tbsp olive oil
1 tbsp cumin seeds
4–6 sub rolls
4 tbsp crème fraîche or cream cheese
2 tbsp mayonnaise
1 tsp mustard

The green sauce
100g leafy fresh green herbs (I used a mix of parsley, coriander, dill and chives)
zest and juice of 1–2 lemons
2 tbsp capers, roughly chopped
50ml olive oil, plus more if needed
salt and black pepper

1   Preheat the oven to 200°C/180°C fan/gas 6.

2   Cut your carrots and parsnips into batons; slice the beetroot into 1cm slices and the celeriac into 1cm half-moons and then into quarters. Add the carrots, parsnips and celeriac to a roasting tin and toss with 1 tablespoon of the olive oil and half the cumin seeds. Add the beetroot to another roasting tray and toss with the remaining olive oil and cumin. Roast the veg for about 45 minutes, until very soft on the inside and crispy on the outside; you should be able to poke a fork easily into the veg.

3   Meanwhile, in a food processor or blender, blitz the herbs, lemon zest and juice and the capers to make a thick paste. Stir through the olive oil. Season with salt and black pepper, adding more lemon juice and/or olive oil if required.

4   Slice your sub rolls in half horizontally. In a small bowl, mix together the crème fraîche with the mayonnaise and mustard. Spread the rolls with the creamy mixture, pile the vegetables on top, then drizzle with the green sauce. Top with the other half of the sub rolls, pressing them down, then cut into quarters. Eat immediately or wrap up and take on a picnic!

Tip You can keep the roasted veg, stored separately, in the fridge for the next day.

 4–6
 10 mins
 45 mins
 Up to 1 day

Super 'Meatball' Sliders

Burgers are one of the dishes people often say they miss the most when they switch to a plant-based diet, but these tasty sliders prove you can still enjoy all those delicious flavours! Perfect for parties, get-togethers and big events with friends and family. Liquid smoke adds a chargrilled taste but it's not essential to the recipe – or you can cook them on the barbecue instead. These are great packed into the Potato Rolls on page 38.

225g chestnut mushrooms, finely chopped
1 x 400g tin cannellini beans, drained and rinsed
1 small onion, finely chopped
4 garlic cloves, finely grated
150–175g breadcrumbs (home-made from a stale loaf)
30g fresh parsley, finely chopped
½ tsp dried rosemary
¼ tsp fennel seeds
1 tsp Worcestershire sauce
1 tbsp soy sauce or tamari
½ tsp liquid smoke
3 tbsp vegetable oil
270g prepared tomato sauce or passata (or my Simplest Tomato Sauce, page 87)
12 bread rolls
115g mozzarella, shredded
2 tbsp butter, melted
1 tbsp grated parmesan
½ tsp sugar
salt and black pepper

Tips If you need gluten-free sliders, ensure you use gluten-free bread and breadcrumbs, and tamari rather than soy sauce.

Look for vegan Worcestershire sauce if you prefer.

1 In a food processor, pulse the mushrooms, beans, onion, 3 garlic cloves, 150g breadcrumbs, parsley (reserving 1 tablespoon for the topping), rosemary, fennel seeds, Worcestershire sauce, soy sauce, liquid smoke and ½ teaspoon each of salt and black pepper until combined, but go slowly so that the mixture doesn't turn mushy. If it seems a little mushy, add some more breadcrumbs.

2 Line a baking sheet or large plate with baking parchment. Roll the mushroom mixture into 12 golf-ball-sized pieces, place them on the lined baking sheet or plate, then chill in the fridge to firm up for 30–45 minutes.

3 Preheat the oven to 180°C/160°C fan/gas 4. Line a 33 x 23cm roasting tin with baking parchment.

4 Heat the vegetable oil in a large frying pan over medium–high heat until shimmering. Carefully place the balls in the pan and cook for about 10 minutes, until browned all over. Pour in the tomato sauce or passata and cook for a further 2 minutes, gently stirring to coat the balls.

5 Slice the bread rolls in half and place the bottom halves on the lined roasting tin. Place one meatball on each half with 2–3 tablespoons of the sauce, then add the mozzarella (about 1 tablespoon on each roll). Cover with the tops of the rolls.

6 In a small bowl, combine the melted butter, parmesan, sugar and the remaining garlic and parsley. Season with salt and black pepper. Brush the tops of the rolls with the sweet and salty butter mixture.

7 Bake in the oven for 15 minutes, or until the bread is golden brown. Remove from the oven and leave to cool slightly before serving.

 12 sliders

 20 mins, plus 30+ mins chilling

 30 mins

 1–2 days

 Up to 1 month

Nut Roast Cake with All the Trimmings

I first made this nut roast when we were visiting family at Christmas. My wife and I were the only vegans in the house, but there wasn't enough for us to have seconds as the plate was wiped clean! Now I always make three so we can finally enjoy leftovers on Boxing Day. It's definitely a crowd-pleaser for vegans and non-vegans alike.

500g carrots, preferably heritage, halved lengthways and cut into 5–7cm batons
2 sweet potatoes
3 tbsp olive oil
30g butter
200g mushrooms, sliced
2 garlic cloves, finely chopped
1 tbsp ground coriander
1 tsp ground cinnamon
1 tsp grated nutmeg
1 tsp ground cumin
a few sprigs fresh thyme
2 tbsp flaxseed or chia seeds
100g mixed nuts, toasted
200g packet of quick-cook mixed grains
1 x 400g tin brown lentils, drained and rinsed
1 tbsp Marmite
3 tbsp fresh parsley, roughly chopped
3 tbsp fresh sage, roughly chopped
2 tbsp nutritional yeast
100g breadcrumbs
salt and black pepper

To serve
Best Roast Potatoes (page 33) (I'd probably make double the quantity!)
roasted Brussels sprouts
gravy
cranberry sauce

1 Preheat the oven to 220°C/200°C fan/gas mark 7.

2 On a baking tray, rub the carrots and sweet potatoes with a little of the olive oil and some salt. Cook in the oven for 35–40 minutes, or until very soft.

3 Meanwhile, heat the remaining olive oil and butter in a large frying pan over a high heat. Once hot, add the sliced mushrooms and a big pinch of salt and a crack of black pepper. Fry for 5–7 minutes until all the liquid has been released from the mushrooms and they're soft and golden. Add the garlic and spices, cook for 1 minute, stir in the thyme, then tip into a large bowl.

4 In a small bowl, mix the flaxseed with 3 tablespoons of water and set aside until it turns into a jelly-like consistency.

5 Put half the toasted nuts in a food processor or blender along with half of the mixed grains, half of the lentils, a splash of water and the Marmite, and blitz into a paste. Roughly chop the remaining nuts and add them to the mushrooms, along with the remaining grains and lentils.

6 When the sweet potato is cooked, add 1½ potatoes to the blender and blitz again. Roughly chop the remaining half a potato, and add to the mushrooms. Preheat the oven to 180°C/160°C fan/gas 4.

Continued $\longrightarrow$

8

20 min

1 hour 55 mins
–2 hours 5 min

Up to 1 week

Up to 1 month

Continued $\longrightarrow$

7   Grab a large springform cake tin, about 23cm diameter. Line the base with a circle of baking parchment. Lay the carrots, cut-side down, on the base of the tin (I like to lie them in alternating directions to ensure as few gaps as possible).

8   Combine the flaxseed mixture and the chopped herbs with the mushrooms, then add the blender mixture, along with the nutritional yeast and breadcrumbs. Stir everything together; the mixture should be thick. Tip into the cake tin, being careful not to move the carrots too much. Tap the base of the tin on a flat surface to make sure everything is pressed into the tin.

9   Cover with foil and bake for 1 hour. Remove the foil and cook for a further 20–25 minutes, until evenly golden. Remove from the oven and allow to cool a little, then turn out onto a plate. Peel back the baking parchment to reveal the amazing carrot surface. Slice and serve with all the roast dinner trimmings.

Tips You can prep the mixture in advance and pull everything together in the morning.

It's freezer friendly too: make it up to a month in advance, then whack it in the oven to heat through on the day.

It's best if your carrots aren't too thick for this.

Grains

Buttery Herb Stuffing

I've found that stuffing recipes often have loads of complicated steps, so this one cuts out all the faff – and uses up leftover bread in the process. Easy to pull together and flavoured with an abundance of fresh herbs, it takes (some of) the stress out of festive cooking. If you have any leftovers, check out the stuffed mushroom recipe on page 246.

450g sourdough (or other) bread,
  torn into 2–3cm pieces
125g butter
150g celery (about 5 sticks),
  finely chopped
150g onion, finely chopped
4 garlic cloves, finely chopped
120ml dry white wine
2 tbsp freshly chopped rosemary
2 tbsp freshly chopped thyme
2 tbsp freshly chopped sage
240ml veg stock
80ml cold water
2 tbsp cornflour
salt and black pepper

1   Preheat the oven to its lowest setting. Place the bread on a baking sheet and bake for 15 minutes, or until the bread is dried out on the surface.

2   Melt the butter in a frying pan over medium heat. Add the celery and onion and cook for about 10 minutes, stirring occasionally, until soft. Stir in the garlic and cook for 1 minute, until fragrant. Add the wine and herbs, increase the heat to bring the wine to a simmer and cook for 5 minutes, until reduced. Add the veg stock, bring to a simmer and cook for 5 minutes.

3   Meanwhile, in a small bowl, stir the water and cornflour together until there are no clumps.

4   Stir the cornflour mixture into the stock and cook for 1–2 minutes, until the mixture thickens slightly. Remove from the heat.

5   Increase the oven temperature to 180°C/160°C fan/gas 4.

6   Put the dried bread in a large baking dish and pour over the onion and celery mixture. Stir until the bread is evenly coated and season with salt and black pepper. Cover with foil and bake for 20 minutes. Remove the foil and bake for a further 18–20 minutes, until dried out on top and crispy around the edges.

7   Remove from the oven and leave to cool slightly before serving.

Tips Skip the first step and let the bread dry out 2–3 days in advance.

Use gluten-free bread if you prefer.

 8
 15 mins
 1 hour 20 mins
 Up to 7 days
 Up to 3 months

Rich Ribollita

This classic Italian soup is traditionally made from leftovers, which is music to my stomach! A hug in a bowl, every mouthful fills you with warmth, love and goodness. It's very flexible - any kind of beans will work, add sweet potato or pumpkin or regular potatoes, stir in spinach at the end, swap celery for fennel... Make it your own with whatever you have knocking around. Great as leftovers the next day too - and, most importantly, it is freezer friendly.

340g sourdough (or other) bread,
  torn or cut into large chunks
6 tbsp extra-virgin olive oil, plus more
  for drizzling
1 onion, chopped
3 carrots, cut into 1cm pieces
2 celery sticks, cut into 1cm pieces
4 garlic cloves, thinly sliced
2 x 400g tins chopped tomatoes
1 tbsp tomato purée
½ tsp chilli flakes
½ tsp dried thyme
½ tsp dried oregano
2 x 400g tins cannellini beans, drained
  and rinsed
950ml veg stock
small bunch of kale, leaves stripped
  from stems and roughly chopped
salt and black pepper
30g parmesan, grated, to serve

1 Preheat the oven to 180°C/160°C fan/gas 4.

2 Toss the bread with 3 tablespoons of olive oil, then season with salt and pepper. Gently squeeze the bread to allow the oil to work into all the nooks and crannies. Bake for 8–10 minutes, until the bread is crispy and golden brown around the edges.

3 Meanwhile, heat the remaining olive oil in a large ovenproof casserole or saucepan over medium heat. Add the onion, carrots, celery and garlic and cook, stirring occasionally, for about 8–10 minutes, until all the vegetables are soft. Season with salt.

4 Add the tomatoes, tomato purée and chilli flakes and cook, stirring often, for 8–10 minutes, until slightly thickened. Add the dried thyme and oregano, cannellini beans and veg stock, bring to a simmer and cook for 5–7 minutes, stirring occasionally. Stir in the kale and cook for about 5 minutes, until the kale is very soft and wilted.

5 Add 1–2 large handfuls of the crunchy bread, stir, then season to taste with salt and pepper. Ladle into bowls, topped with more of the crunchy bread, a drizzle of olive oil and some grated parmesan.

Tips This can be made in an instant pot, slow cooker or on the hob.

*To make in advance - or to store leftovers - don't add the crunchy bread until ready to eat.

Use gluten-free bread if you prefer.

Use the kale stems for Fridge Greens Fusilli (page 160) or Stems and Herbs Pesto (page 156).

 4 15 mins 30 mins 1–2 days* Up to 1 month

Brown Butter and Crispy Sage Mac and Peas

This is an adult version of everyone's childhood favourite mac and cheese! The puffed cereal and breadcrumbs give it an incredible texture on top. Perfect as a midweek dinner or serve as a side dish.

60g any type of bread
  (preferably slightly stale)
60g butter
30g plain flour
730ml milk (I use oat)
450g macaroni or pasta shells
125g cheddar cheese
75g frozen peas
20g puffed rice cereal, crushed
3 tbsp freshly chopped parsley
3 tbsp olive oil
salt and black pepper

Brown butter sage sauce
60g butter
3 tbsp roughly chopped fresh sage

Tips It's best to use bread that is not baked fresh that day.

Keep the crusts on the bread to waste less.

Breadcrumbs can be made in advance and kept in the freezer.

1   Preheat the oven to 150°C/130°C fan/gas 2.

2   Blitz the bread in a food processor for a few seconds to a crumb texture. Spread the crumbs on a baking sheet in a single layer and bake for 8–10 minutes, until lightly toasted and dry. Remove from the oven and set aside.

3   Meanwhile, melt the butter in a large saucepan over medium heat. Add the flour, whisking continuously, and cook for 1 minute. Whisk in the milk and bring to the boil, then reduce the heat and simmer for 8–10 minutes, stirring often, to a silky, glossy sauce. Season, then remove from the heat.

4   Meanwhile, bring a large pan of water to the boil and cook the macaroni for 4 minutes. Drain well.

5   Increase the oven temperature to 200°C/180°C fan/gas 6.

6   Toss the macaroni and three-quarters of the cheddar in a shallow baking dish. Pour over the sauce (do not stir) and cover with foil. Bake for about 15 minutes, until the macaroni is slightly tender.

7   Meanwhile, make the brown butter. Heat the butter in a frying pan over medium heat. Add the sage and cook for 3–5 minutes, stirring occasionally, until the butter turns brown and has a nutty aroma. Remove from the heat.

8   Place the frozen peas in a colander and run under hot water for 30 seconds, then drain and set aside until dry. Toss the peas in the sage butter and set aside.

9   In a bowl, toss the breadcrumbs and crushed cereal with the parsley and olive oil.

10 Remove the foil. Sprinkle over the remaining cheddar, pour over the brown butter and peas and scatter the breadcrumbs. Bake, uncovered, for 8–10 minutes, until the edges start bubbling and the top is golden. Cool slightly before serving.

 4–8   15 mins   40 mins   Up to 5 days   Up to 3 months

BYOB (Build Your Own Bruschetta)

Easy to make and one of my favourite ways to use up leftover bread and tomatoes, these can be assembled on the spot – and I love getting other people involved in cooking! A little different from a traditional bruschetta, I've added white beans for a chunky texture. To lift the sweetness, try a handful of strawberries or raspberries too.

1 large crusty baguette
4–6 garlic cloves
handful of fresh basil and mint,
  to serve
good olive oil, to drizzle

Balsamic tomatoes
1 small red onion
zest and juice of 1 lemon
2 tbsp thick balsamic vinegar
100g sundried tomatoes
200g cherry tomatoes
200g heritage tomatoes
1 x 400g tin white beans, rinsed
  and drained
salt and black pepper

1   Make the balsamic tomatoes. Finely chop the red onion and add to a bowl with the lemon zest and juice, the balsamic vinegar and a big pinch of salt.

2   Roughly chop the sundried tomatoes and add to the mixture. Halve the cherry tomatoes and roughly chop the heritage tomatoes and add both to the bowl. Add the white beans and season with salt and black pepper. Set the tomato mixture in the middle of the table ready for people to start assembling their bruschetta.

3   Heat the grill to high. Slice the baguette on an angle and grill the slices for 2–3 minutes on each side, until golden brown. Arrange on a plate and put on the table.

4   Now for the fun part: let everyone use the peeled garlic to rub down their bread, before piling high with the tomato mixture and scattering with fresh herbs. Finally pass around a nice bottle of olive oil so people can drizzle it all over their bruschetta.

Tips   Add a small handful of fresh strawberries or fresh raspberries to intensify the sweetness of the tomatoes.

Sub the baguette for gluten-free bread if you desire.

 4–6   10 mins   5 mins   Up to 3 days

Sourdough French Toast with Glazed Peaches

When I eat a peach, I always feel as though time seems to slow down. You can't rush eating peaches – they're too juicy and delicious! Griddled with maple syrup, they create a beautiful sticky glaze to serve on top of cinnamon French toast. Change the fruits with the seasons so you can enjoy this all year round – try it with bananas or stewed berries and apples.

2 tbsp plain flour
1 tbsp flaxseed meal
1 tsp ground cinnamon
¼ tsp grated nutmeg
1 tsp vanilla extract
1 tbsp sugar
250ml oat milk
3 peaches, stones removed and
  cut into wedges
2–3 tbsp maple syrup
4 tbsp butter
4 slices of sourdough

To serve
1–2 tbsp yoghurt per serving
  (I use coconut)
½ tsp icing sugar per serving
¼ tsp ground cinnamon per serving

1 In a large bowl, whisk the flour, flaxseed, cinnamon, nutmeg, vanilla extract and sugar until combined. Slowly pour in the oat milk, still whisking, to make a very thin batter with no streaks of flour. Set aside.

2 Heat a griddle pan or large frying pan over a high heat. Line the pan with a piece of baking paper and add the peachwedges. Cook for 6–8 mins, turning halfway, until softened and a little charred. Drizzle the maple syrup over the peaches in the pan, then remove from the heat and transfer to a plate with the paper. (Depending on the size of your pan, you might have to do this in batches).

3 In a large frying pan, heat 2 tablespoons of the butter over a medium–high heat. Dip 2 of the sourdough slices in the batter, really drenching them through, then cook in the butter for 2–3 minutes on each, until golden and slightly crispy. Repeat with the remaining butter and slices of bread.

4 Top the French toast with the glazed peaches and a dollop of coconut yoghurt. Sprinkle with a little cinnamon and icing sugar to finish.

Tips Experiment with whatever bread you have left over: bagels, croissants, even doughnuts!

Best served hot!

 4
 5 mins
 10– 15 mins
 1 week
 Up to 1 month

3– Nightshades

Tomato
Aubergine
Pepper

One-pan Lasagne

If you have Italian heritage, you'll know that breaking pasta is basically blasphemy. But I won't tell if you won't! This one-pan wonder shortcuts your way to a creamy, satisfying beautiful lasagne in less than half the time – plus less washing up too. Sometimes, life is just too short to layer up lasagne sheets. Keep an eye on the heat and don't have it too high as it could dry out the pasta before it's cooked through – add a splash or two of water if necessary.

2 tbsp olive oil
1 onion, finely chopped
2 tbsp freshly chopped basil,
    plus stems, chopped separately
2 garlic cloves, finely grated
200g cooked beluga or Puy
    lentils (tinned are fine)
100g walnuts, chopped
2 tbsp tomato purée
1 x 400g tin chopped tomatoes
125ml oat milk
125ml water or veg stock
180g dried lasagne sheets
1½ tsp freshly chopped oregano
50g parmesan, grated
salt and black pepper
Cheesy Garlic Bread (page 199),
    to serve

1   Heat the olive oil in a large skillet or heavy-based frying pan over medium heat. Add the onion and basil stems and cook for 5–7 minutes, stirring occasionally, until soft, then season with salt and pepper.

2   Add the garlic, lentils and walnuts, stir and cook for a further 2 minutes. Add the tomato purée and cook for 1–2 minutes, stirring often, until the mixture thickens and begins to stick to the pan. Stir in the tomatoes, milk and water.

3   Break the lasagne sheets in half and then in half again. Add the broken lasagne to the sauce, stirring, a little at a time so that they don't cling together. Then reduce the heat and cook, stirring often, for 15–20 minutes or until the pasta is al dente.

4   Divide the lasagne between 4 bowls or plates and sprinkle with fresh basil, oregano and parmesan. Serve with my cheesy garlic bread.

Tip Use gluten-free pasta
if you prefer.

 4   10 mins   25–35 mins   1–2 days   Up to 1 month

Speedy Cherry Tomato Fettuccine

My mum's tomato sauce is incredible, but it's an all-day affair, starting at 7am on a Saturday and filling the house with slowly roasting onions and garlic until late afternoon. I don't want to be at the stove all day, and so this quick and easy cherry tomato pasta dish with garlic, basil and red pepper flakes is on the table in under 20 minutes!

300g cherry tomatoes
3 tbsp extra-virgin olive oil
2 garlic cloves, finely grated
4 fresh basil sprigs, tender stems
  chopped and leaves separated
¼ tsp red pepper flakes
1 tbsp tomato purée
200g fettuccine
20g parmesan cheese
salt and pepper
approx. 30g Garlic and Lemon
  Pangrattato (page 200),
  to serve

1 Slice half of the cherry tomatoes, leaving the rest of them whole.

2 Warm the olive oil in a saucepan over medium heat. Once the oil is warm, but not burning, add the tomatoes and cook for 5–7 minutes, stirring often, until they have lost some of their shape. Add the grated garlic, basil stems and red pepper flakes. Stir to combine and cook for 1 minute before stirring in the tomato purée. Cook for a further 1 minute, then season with salt and black pepper. Remove from heat.

3 Meanwhile, bring a large saucepan of salted water to a boil. Cook the fettuccine according to the packet directions. Drain the pasta, reserving 5 tablespoons of the pasta cooking water.

4 Return the tomatoes to a low heat, add the fettuccine and stir in 1 tablespoon of the reserved pasta cooking water at a time until the sauce clings to the pasta. Grate in parmesan cheese you go, tossing in between.

5 Serve the pasta hot, divided into bowls, topped with my garlic and lemon pangrattato and the basil leaves.

Tip Grating in the garlic near the end retains its depth so doesn't become too sweet.

 2   5 mins   12 mins   Up to 5 days   Up to 3 months

Simplest Tomato Sauce

This version of home-made sauce takes less than half the time! Grating the tomato first means it's already mostly broken down, so it cooks quickly and results in a much smoother, even sauce. I like to batch cook this sauce in the summer when tomatoes are in abundance. Last year I turned 20kg of tomatoes into sauce and jarred it up to enjoy in the winter.

1kg large ripe tomatoes
1 tbsp extra-virgin olive oil
4 garlic cloves, finely grated
1 tbsp tomato purée
1 bunch of fresh basil,
   stems chopped
1 tbsp butter
salt and black pepper

1   First, you're going to grate the tomatoes. Cut a slice off the end of each tomato and set the sliced-off bits aside. Pressing the cut side of the tomatoes into the largest holes of a box grater, grate them into a large bowl. Finely chop the sliced-off bits and any pieces of tomato that are too difficult to grate and add them to the bowl.

2   Generously season with salt and black pepper. Gently mix through the olive oil, grated garlic, tomato purée and basil stems.

3   Into a large saucepan over medium heat, slowly pour the tomato mixture. Cook for 10–12 minutes, stirring often. Remove from the heat and serve immediately, or store in an airtight container while still warm.

Tips Swap fresh tomatoes for tinned tomatoes, skip the grating and go straight to step 2.

You need only the basil stems for this sauce: use the leaves to garnish when serving with pasta or other dishes.

Make the sauce up to 5 days in advance, or freeze.

  15 mins   20 mins   Up to 5 days   Up to 3 months   **GF**

One-tray Baked Gnocchi

Sometimes when I post a new recipe on social media, it really seems to resonate with how everyone's feeling – and this dish was one of those! With millions of views on Instagram, I can see why it's so popular. It's basically a deluxe version of a pasta bake – simple cooking and easy to serve up, with all the flavours merging together as the pasta gets slightly crispy. Try it with your favourite ravioli or tortellini too.

400g gnocchi
3 tbsp extra-virgin olive oil
325g cherry tomatoes, chopped
75g mozzarella, shredded
3 tbsp freshly chopped basil,
  plus stems, chopped separately
4 sausages, cut into 2–3cm pieces
4 garlic cloves, finely grated
60g leafy greens (e.g. spinach, kale,
  Swiss chard), roughly chopped
salt and black pepper

1   Preheat the oven to 200°C/180°C fan/gas 6.

2   Place the gnocchi in a large bowl, cover with boiling water and leave for 2 minutes. Stir, then drain thoroughly.

3   Add the gnocchi to a large roasting tin, drizzle with the olive oil, then add the tomatoes, mozzarella, basil stems, sausages, garlic and leafy greens. Toss to combine and season with salt and black pepper.

4   Bake for 20 minutes, until the gnocchi are slightly charred around the edges. Remove from the oven and leave to cool for a few minutes before serving.

5   Serve in bowls, sprinkled with chopped basil.

Tips Swap gnocchi for tortellini or ravioli.

It's also great as leftovers.

 4
 10 mins
 20 mins
 1–3 days
 Up to 1 month

Tomato Salad, Tofu Whip and Garlicky Crumbs

Juicy tomatoes, crunchy garlicky crumbs and a creamy tofu dressing, I just can't get enough of this in the summer when tomatoes are at their peak. Simple, fresh flavours and subtle heat from the Dijon mustard let the tomatoes shine in all their glory as the stars of the show.

1 kg mixed tomatoes,
  preferably heritage
2 slices of sourdough bread
  (stale bread is better)
2 tbsp olive oil
2 garlic cloves, minced
40g capers
zest of 1 lemon
1 tbsp roughly chopped
  fresh parsley
salt
30g parmesan,
  shaved, to serve

Tofu whip
240g silken tofu
3 tbsp nutritional yeast
1 tbsp miso paste
juice of 1 lemon
black pepper

1 Slice the tomatoes and place on a large plate. Season with salt.

2 In a food processor, blitz the bread to form breadcrumbs. Heat a large frying pan over medium heat and dry fry the breadcrumbs for 2 minutes to remove any moisture. Add the oil and stir to coat the breadcrumbs. Add the garlic and capers, fry for about 2 minutes until golden brown, then transfer to a bowl. Season with salt and stir through the lemon zest and parsley.

3 In a food processor, blend the ingredients for the tofu whip until smooth and slightly thick. Season with salt and black pepper.

4 Spread the whipped tofu on a large platter, arrange the tomatoes on top and scatter with shaved parmesan and the herby zesty garlicky breadcrumbs.

 4

 10 mins

 5 mins

 Up to 5 days

Salted Tomato and Cheese Toasties

This takes grilled cheese sandwiches up a notch. Salting and draining the tomatoes and sliding them into your cooked sandwich just before serving removes some of the moisture and firms up the tomato, meaning you won't end up with a soggy sandwich and a burning hot tomato slice inside. It also enhances the true sweetness of the tomato.

2 large beefsteak or heirloom
  tomatoes, thinly sliced
280g cheddar cheese, grated
60g pepper jack or other
  chilli-flavoured cheese, grated
8 slices sourdough (or other) bread
4 tbsp butter, softened
4 tbsp mayo
salt and black pepper

1 Place the tomato slices in a single layer on a wire rack set over a roasting tin. Season with a generous pinch of salt, then leave for 20 minutes to release some of their juices, flipping them over halfway through. Pat the tomato slices dry just before serving.

2 Mix the cheeses to combine evenly.

3 Heat a large frying pan over low heat. Spread 2 slices of bread with butter on one side, then place them butter-side down in the frying pan. Spread both slices with mayonnaise, then sprinkle a quarter of the cheeses on top of each slice. Spread a layer of mayonnaise on 2 more slices of bread, then gently press them down on top of the cheese, closing the sandwiches. Cook for about 8 minutes, pressing down with a wide spatula, until the bottom is golden brown. Spread the top of each sandwich with butter, then carefully flip them over and cook until golden brown and crispy.

4 Transfer the sandwiches to plates, then carefully lift up the top slices of bread and insert a few slices of tomato. Press the top slices of bread down lightly again to close the sandwiches and cut them in half.

5 Repeat to make 2 more sandwiches.

Tips How to make the perfect tomato and cheese toasties:

Salt your tomatoes to remove excess liquid; pat them dry and add them just before serving.

Grate the cheeses, for faster and more even melting.

Use gluten-free bread if you prefer.

Quick Gazpacho

Although I'm usually more of a hot-tomato-soup-and-grilled-cheese-sandwich kind of guy, when the sun's out, I always turn to this refreshing chilled gazpacho to cool me down. Nectarine brings out the sweetness of the tomatoes and perfectly balances all the flavours. Go ahead and serve it with the Cheese Toastie on page 93 for a hot-cold contrast.

1 cucumber
400g very ripe tomatoes, quartered
1 large red pepper, seeded
  and quartered
1 large ripe nectarine,
  stone removed, halved
1 small shallot, chopped
2 garlic cloves, finely grated
2 tbsp sherry vinegar
3 tbsp extra-virgin olive oil, plus
  more for drizzling
salt and black pepper

To serve
60g cherry tomatoes, thinly sliced
snipped fresh chives

1 Very finely slice 5cm of the cucumber and set aside for a garnish. Roughly chop the remaining cucumber and place in a large bowl with the 400g tomatoes, red pepper, nectarine, shallot, garlic, vinegar and 1 teaspoon of salt. Gently toss together, then chill in the fridge for at least 30 minutes and up to 4 hours for the flavours to infuse.

2 Carefully add the contents of the bowl, including all the juices, to a high-speed blender. Add the olive oil and blend on medium–high speed until smooth. Strain through a wide-mesh sieve into a large bowl or container then chill for at least 30 minutes, or until ready to serve.

3 Serve the gazpacho, topped with sliced cherry tomatoes, the reserved cucumber slices, chives and a drizzle of olive oil. Season with salt and black pepper.

Tip Can be made 1 day in advance; cover and chill.

 4   10 mins   Up to 3 days   **GF**

Tomato, Feta and Crushed Almond Salad

This is my take on the classic Greek salad, refreshing and full of flavour. As this salad doesn't have tender greens, it's a good one to make in advance and keep in the fridge. Perfect for a picnic in the sun or an easy lunch to take to work.

200g feta
1 tbsp freshly chopped oregano
1 tbsp freshly chopped parsley
2 tbsp olive oil
1 large green pepper, seeded, sliced into 2cm pieces
1 small red onion, very thinly sliced
1 baby cucumber, quartered lengthways, then chopped
400g mixed baby tomatoes, halved
35g pitted kalamata olives, halved
1 tbsp freshly chopped mint
2 tbsp balsamic or red wine vinegar
salt and black pepper

To serve
zest of 1 lemon
4 tbsp almonds, toasted and crushed

1 Break the feta into chunks in a bowl, then add the oregano, parsley and 1 tablespoon of the olive oil. Season with a small pinch of salt and black pepper, then gently turn the feta to coat in the herby oil.

2 Heat the remaining oil in a frying pan over medium–high heat, add the green pepper and cook for about 8 minutes, until slightly softened and just starting to colour. Remove from the pan from the heat and use a slotted spoon or tongs to lift out the pepper. Set aside to cool for 5–10 minutes, reserving the oil.

3 In another mixing bowl, mix together the onion, cucumber, tomatoes, olives, mint, vinegar and a generous pinch of salt. Gently fold through the green pepper. Serve the salad on a serving plate or divided into bowls, topped with the feta and lemon zest, toasted and crushed almonds and drizzled with the reserved oil.

Tips More bulk? Add roasted chickpeas or crispy tofu.

Making ahead? Sprinkle with a few fresh mint leaves just before serving.

 6 10 mins 10 mins Up to 5 days Up to 1 month **GF**

Harissa Aubergine Kebabs with Zing Zing Grain Salad

A summery salad with barbecue vibes, this is crunchy, sweet and bursting with big flavours and textures from tomatoes, cucumber, fresh herbs, sumac, lemon and pomegranate. The hero though is the charred aubergine pieces, which are brushed with a spicy and sweet harissa and maple glaze and cooked until meltingly soft and sticky.

3 aubergines (or 2 large)
1 red onion, finely sliced
2 lemons
1 tsp sumac
1 tbsp maple syrup
2 tbsp harissa paste
200g bulgur wheat
250g cherry tomatoes, halved
1 cucumber, cut into 1cm cubes
150g pomegranate seeds
handful of fresh herbs (I used parsley and mint), roughly chopped
3 tbsp olive oil
salt and black pepper
2 tbsp toasted sesame seeds, to serve

1   Preheat the grill to high. Cut the aubergine into large chunks – around 4cm pieces. Line a tray with foil, spread out the aubergine pieces and grill for 10–15 minutes, until charred.

2   Meanwhile, put the onion slices in the base of a large bowl. Add the zest and juice of 1 lemon, the sumac, 1 teaspoon of the maple syrup and a big pinch of salt. Use your hands to scrunch everything together and then set aside so the onion can lightly pickle.

3   Mix the harissa with 3–4 tablespoons of water so it emulsifies into a sauce. Add the remaining maple syrup, season with salt and black pepper, and mix well.

4   Once the aubergine is charred, remove from the oven and increase the heat to 220°C/200°C fan/gas 7. Carefully slide the aubergine chunks onto skewers, lay them on the tray and either brush or spoon over the harissa mixture. Cover with foil and cook for 10–15 minutes, until very soft, removing the foil for the last 5 minutes so they become sticky.

5   While they cook, bring a saucepan of salted water to the boil, add the bulgur wheat and cook according to the packet instructions. Add the remaining ingredients for the salad into the large bowl with the pickled onion.

6   Drain and rinse the bulgur wheat in cold water, then add to the salad bowl and toss together. Taste, and season with salt and black pepper. Cut the remaining lemon into wedges. Spoon the salad into bowls, top with the aubergine skewers, scatter with sesame seeds and serve with lemon wedges on the side.

Tips If you're cooking for friends in the summer, cook the aubergine on the barbecue!

The salad will keep for up to 3 days in the fridge.

 4   20 mins   20–30 mins   Up to 3 days   Up to 1 month

Charred Aubergine and Peanut Stew

My good friend Rachel Ama makes the most delicious sweet potato West African stew, and I took inspiration from it to make this charred and smoky aubergine version. Rich, spicy, creamy, salty, sharp and sweet, it has everything going on!

1–2 medium aubergines, chopped
   into 2.5cm pieces
4 tbsp groundnut oil, plus more
   if needed
1 onion, quartered
2 garlic cloves
30g fresh ginger
2 tbsp fresh coriander, stalks chopped
   and leaves reserved for a garnish
1 tsp ground coriander
1 tsp smoked paprika
½ tsp ground cumin
1 x 400g tin chopped tomatoes
2 tbsp tomato purée
½ tsp salt
¼ tsp black pepper
500ml veg stock
125g peanut butter, either crunchy
   or smooth
rice or flatbreads, to serve

Pink onions
1 small red onion, sliced
1 tbsp granulated sugar
2 tbsp red wine vinegar or apple
   cider vinegar

Tips Best served with fluffy rice or my Fragrant Flatbreads on page 206.

It may sound counterintuitive to soak the aubergines first, but it softens them up so you can squeeze out more of their liquid.

1 In a large mixing bowl, soak the aubergine pieces in warm water for 20 minutes.

2 After 20 minutes of soaking, the aubergine should be soft. Squeeze the aubergine to release its natural water. (It sounds crazy and a total waste of time, but it's better than adding salt to draw out the water – trust me!)

3 Heat 2 tablespoons of the oil in a frying pan over medium heat. Once warm, add the aubergine, flesh-side down. Leave, undisturbed for 3–4 minutes, until slightly charred. Stirring occasionally, cook for a further 5 minutes, until browned on all sides.

4 Meanwhile, in a food processor, blend the onion, garlic, ginger, coriander stalks and spices to a paste consistency.

5 When the aubergine is cooked, transfer to a plate and wipe the pan clean. Heat the remaining 2 tablespoons of the oil in the frying pan over medium heat. Once warm, add the paste, stirring often, and cook for 5–7 minutes, adding more oil if the paste starts to stick.

6 Add the aubergine, chopped tomatoes and tomato purée, and fry, stirring for about 1 minute. Season with the salt and black pepper. Add the veg stock and peanut butter and mix well. Simmer over medium heat for 15–20 minutes, stirring occasionally, until you have a thick sauce.

7 While the stew is cooking, put the sliced red onion in a small bowl. Add the granulated sugar and vinegar and stir well. Set aside to pickle lightly.

8 Serve the stew with fluffy rice or flatbreads, topped with the pink onions and coriander leaves.

 4   10 mins   30–40 mins   Up to 3 days   Up to 1 month   **GF**

Really Good Stuffed Peppers

Stuffed peppers may have a bit of a Seventies vibe about them but there's a reason they're still so popular – they're delicious! They're also very versatile. These have a strong taste of the Mediterranean from pine nuts, couscous, feta, olives and sultanas, rounded off with a harissa-tahini dressing. Just like flares and denim-on-denim, these never go out of fashion for long!

olive oil, for brushing
4 mixed peppers, or romano peppers, halved and seeded
200g couscous
2 garlic cloves, chopped
250–300ml boiling veg stock
16 pitted green olives, chopped
1 tbsp capers
50g feta, crumbled, plus more for topping
30g pine nuts, toasted
20g sultanas
zest of 1 lemon
2 tbsp freshly chopped mint, plus more to serve
2 tbsp freshly chopped parsley, plus more to serve
2 tbsp freshly chopped dill, plus more to serve
salt and black pepper

Harissa-tahini dressing
1 tbsp harissa
2 tbsp tahini
1 tbsp olive oil
1 tsp lemon juice

1 Preheat the oven to 180°C/160°C fan/gas 4. Line a baking sheet with baking parchment and brush with olive oil.

2 Place the peppers on the baking sheet and cook in the oven for 15 minutes, until they are beginning to soften and are slightly charred around the edges.

3 Meanwhile, put the couscous and garlic in a heatproof bowl and pour in boiling veg stock to cover the couscous by 2–3cm. Cover the bowl with a clean tea towel and set aside for 10–15 minutes, until the couscous is soft and fluffy.

4 Add all the remaining filling ingredients, season to taste with salt and pepper and mix well.

5 Scoop the couscous mixture into the cooked peppers, topping with more feta. Bake for 10 minutes, until the peppers are soft and the filling lightly crisp and golden.

6 While they are cooking, make the harissa-tahini dressing by mixing the ingredients in a small bowl until smooth. If the sauce is too thick, add a splash of water to help loosen.

7 Remove the stuffed peppers from the oven and let them cool for a few minutes before serving. Drizzle the dressing on top and scatter with fresh herbs.

Tip These can be served cold. Prepare 1 day in advance, cover and keep chilled.

 4–8
 10 mins
 25 mins
 Up to 3 days
 Up to 1 month
GF

Spicy Red Pepper Dip and Crispy Harissa Mince

This is my interpretation of an amazing dish, muhammara, a spicy Middle Eastern red pepper and walnut dip. It's very easy to pull together, especially if you use a jar of roasted peppers. I've topped mine with crispy harissa mince for a more complete meal, but if you leave it out it's perfect for parties, served with crudites or pitta breads, or spread on the inside of sandwiches, like my Roasted Root Veg Sub Rolls on page 66.

2 tbsp olive oil, plus more to drizzle
1 onion, finely diced
400g mince
1 garlic clove, minced
2 tbsp harissa paste
handful of fresh parsley
handful of fresh dill
salt and black pepper

Muhammara
100g walnuts
400g jar of roasted red peppers
   (350 drained weight), drained,
   or 4–5 red peppers, roasted
   (see Tip, below)
4 tbsp olive oil
juice of 1 lemon
1 tsp smoked paprika

To serve
1 lemon, cut into wedges
4–8 Fragrant Flatbreads (page 206)
   or rice

1   In a large frying pan, dry toast the walnuts for about 5 minutes over medium heat, occasionally shaking the pan, until the walnuts are fragrant and toasted. Remove from the pan and set aside.

2   Using the same frying pan, heat the 2 tablespoons of olive oil over a medium heat, and fry the onion with a generous pinch of salt and black pepper, stirring often until very soft. Add the mince and turn the heat up slightly. Cook for 5–7 minutes, stirring occasionally, until the mixture is browned and crispy. Add the garlic and cook for a minute further, then spoon in the harissa and combine. Remove from heat and set aside.

3   Reserving 1 tablespoon for a garnish, blitz the toasted walnuts with the rest of the muhammara ingredients in a high-speed blender, until it forms a smooth sauce. Taste and season with salt and pepper, then spread on a big platter using the back of a spoon.

4   Top the sauce with the crispy harissa mince, scatter with the remaining walnuts, chopping them up a little if you want. Finish with fresh herbs, an extra drizzle of olive oil and a crack of black pepper. Serve with flatbreads for scooping it all up, or with rice.

Tip If cooking with fresh red peppers: preheat the oven to 200°C/180°C fan/gas 6. Cut the peppers in half and remove the seeds and stems. Cook on a baking tray for 20–25 minutes, until charred. Remove from oven and cool before removing the charred skin.

 4   10 mins   20 mins   Up to 5 days   Up to 1 month

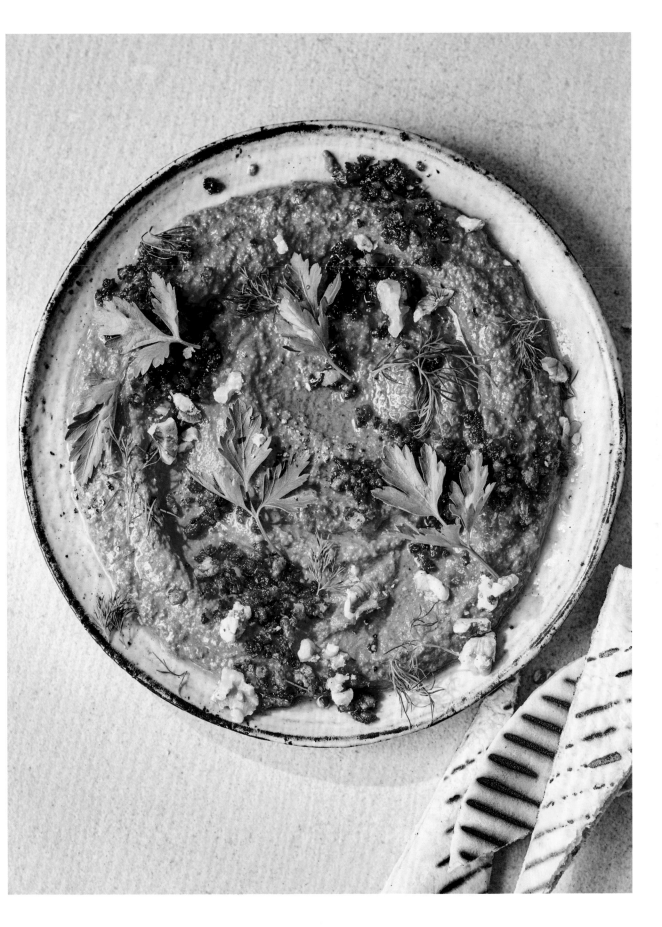

Black Pepper Tofu Stir-fry

Crispy, pan-fried tofu and stir-fried peppers are tossed together in a warm peppery glaze, fiery from the chillies and with an extra tongue-tingling kick from the black pepper. This stir-fry is a weeknight classic in my home, best served with fluffy white rice or noodles. You could also serve it as a side dish, as part of a feast.

Crispy tofu
280g extra-firm tofu, cut into 2cm strips
1 tbsp cornflour
4 tbsp vegetable oil

Black pepper sauce
3 tbsp soy sauce or tamari
2 tbsp black peppercorns, crushed
   (use a mortar and pestle
   or spice grinder)
1 tbsp brown sugar
2 tsp hoisin sauce
2 tsp toasted sesame oil

Stir-fried peppers
1 tbsp vegetable oil
2 red peppers, seeded and cut
   into 2cm squares
1 green pepper, seeded and cut
   into 2cm squares
1 shallot, thinly sliced
2 garlic cloves, finely chopped
1–2 spring onions, thinly sliced
1 tbsp finely chopped fresh ginger
¼ tsp chilli flakes
1 fresh red chilli, thinly sliced

To serve
spring onions, thinly sliced
zest of 1 lime
rice or noodles

Tip If gluten is an issue for you, ensure you use tamari, a gluten-free version of soy sauce, and serve with rice or gluten-free noodles.

1 First, make the sauce. In a mixing bowl, whisk together the soy sauce, crushed black peppercorns, sugar, hoisin sauce and sesame oil. Set aside.

2 To make the crispy tofu, blot the tofu dry, pressing to remove excess water. In a large mixing bowl, toss the tofu with the cornflour until evenly coated.

3 Heat the oil in a large non-stick frying pan over medium heat. Once hot, carefully drop in the tofu, separating the pieces so that they don't stick. Fry, undisturbed, for 2–3 minutes, until golden brown and lightly crispy on one side. Cook for a further 10–12 minutes, stirring occasionally, to fry all sides. Carefully tip the crispy tofu into a colander to drain.

4 Meanwhile, heat another large non-stick frying pan or wok over high heat. Add the oil, reduce the heat to medium–high and add the peppers and shallot. Stir-fry for 4–5 minutes, until the peppers and shallot are soft. Add the garlic, spring onions, ginger, chilli flakes and red chilli and stir-fry for 45 seconds, until the garlic and ginger smell fragrant.

5 For the last minute of cooking, add the crispy tofu to the stir-fried peppers and pour in the sauce, then remove from the heat continuing to stir to coat everything evenly.

6 Serve hot, sprinkled with spring onions and lime zest, with noodles or rice.

 2–4 15 mins 15 mins Up to 3 days Up to 1 month

Sticky Aubergine and Peanut Salad

This is one of my all-time favourite ways to cook aubergine. The trick is to grill the aubergine without any oil for a really intense, smoky, charred flavour. Coated in a sweet, sticky maple-sriracha glaze, it's lip-smackingly good. With a zesty peanut butter dressing, fresh herbs, crunchy peanuts, spring onions and chilli, this has so much going on! Serve with brown or white rice for a satisfying main course.

2 aubergines
2 tbsp soy sauce or tamari
2 tbsp maple syrup
1 tbsp sriracha
2 tbsp sesame oil

Sweet and spicy peanut sauce
2 tbsp peanut butter, either smooth
  or crunchy
1 tbsp sriracha
zest and juice of 1–2 limes
1 tbsp maple syrup

To serve
50g peanuts, roughly chopped
4 tbsp chopped fresh coriander
4 tbsp chopped fresh mint
3 spring onions, thinly sliced
1 red chilli, thinly sliced

1   Preheat the grill as high as it will go. Slice the aubergines in half lengthways and use a knife to cross hatch the flesh. Grill in a roasting tin for 10 minutes or until charred. Once the aubergine is grilled, remove from the oven and turn the oven to 220°C/200°C fan/gas 7.

2   Meanwhile, whisk together the soy, maple syrup, siracha and sesame oil. Place the charred aubergine on a baking sheet lined with baking parchment and drizzle with the marinade. Cover with foil and roast for 20 minutes. Remove the foil cover and spoon any glaze in the tray over the aubergine, then roast for a further 8–10 minutes, uncovered, until very soft and sticky.

3   Whisk the ingredients for the sweet and spicy peanut sauce with enough water to make it drizzleable consistency.

4   Once the aubergines are cooked, place on a large platter and drizzle with the sauce. Scatter over the peanuts, coriander, mint, spring onions and red chilli.

 2

 15 mins

 40 mins

 Up to 5 days

 Up to 1 month

Romesco Risotto

Smoky, charred roasted red peppers and walnut romesco sauce is stirred through risotto to produce this amazing deep red, richly flavoured rice dish. If you have time, go ahead and roast your own peppers, but keeping some in a jar means this dish is a great store-cupboard standby. Serve with a big crunchy green salad.

1 jar roasted red peppers (350g drained weight), or 5 red peppers, roasted (see Tip on page 105)
50g walnuts, toasted, plus more to serve
1.3 litres veg stock, warmed
2 tbsp olive oil, plus more to serve
1 onion, finely chopped
2 garlic cloves, minced
1 tbsp tomato purée
1 tsp smoked paprika
300g risotto rice
150ml white wine
salt and black pepper

To serve
handful of chopped fresh parsley leaves
grated parmesan
zest of 1 lemon

1   Drain the red peppers, reserving the water, then blitz half of the roasted peppers with the toasted walnuts and 50ml of the veg stock. Season well with salt and black pepper. Add the reserved water to the remaining stock. Roughly chop the remaining red peppers.

2   Heat the olive oil in a large high-sided frying pan over medium heat. Add the onion with a big pinch of salt and fry for 5 minutes, until softened. Add the garlic, tomato purée and smoked paprika. Cook for 2 minutes, then add the risotto rice. Stir and cook until the rice starts to make popping sounds.

3   Pour in the white wine and cook, stirring, until it has been absorbed by the rice. Turn the heat down and add the stock, a ladle at a time, stirring until it's all absorbed. Be patient, risotto is best made slowly! Once the stock is all absorbed, stir through the red pepper and walnut sauce. Taste and season with salt and pepper. If the rice is a still a bit chalky, add a splash of water and cook a little longer; the rice should be cooked through with a slight bite. Stir through the chopped red peppers in the final minute of cooking.

4   Spoon into bowls, top with chopped parsley, grated parmesan, a scattering of reserved toasted crushed walnuts, lemon zest, a drizzle of olive oil and a crack of black pepper.

Tips Best served hot!

 4   10 mins   30 mins   1–3 days   Up to 1 month

Ratatouille Grain Bowl

A big hit of veg in one bowl, this is inspired by the classic Provençal dish, which I've made more substantial by serving on garlicky grains. As it cooks in the oven, all the flavours of the veg soften into each other, producing a comforting, rounded dish with a subtle warm-cool contrasting mustard crème fraîche drizzled on top.

2 aubergines
2 red peppers
2 red onions
1 bulb of garlic
4 tbsp olive oil, plus more to drizzle
300g cherry tomatoes
1 tsp dried oregano
250g freekeh or barley (or 2 x 200g pouches of cooked mixed grains)
juice of 1 lemon
handful of fresh parsley, finely chopped
120g crème fraîche
1 tsp Dijon mustard
salt and black pepper

To serve
4 tbsp pine nuts, toasted and roughly chopped
2 tbsp fresh basil leaves, torn

1   Preheat the oven to 200°C/180°C fan/gas 6.

2   Roughly chop your aubergines into 3cm chunks. Cut the tops off the peppers, remove the seeds, then cut into 3cm chunks. Peel the red onions and cut into wedges. Add the prepped veg to a large roasting tray and snuggle in the whole garlic bulb. Drizzle with 2 tablespoons of the olive oil, season well with salt and black pepper, and roast for 20 minutes.

3   Add the tomatoes and dried oregano and roast for a further 20 minutes, until everything is cooked through and soft.

4   Meanwhile, if you're using dried grains, rinse them well and cook in boiling water according to packet instructions. Drain, rinse and tip into a bowl. If you're using precooked grains, run under hot water for 10 seconds, drain well and tip into a bowl. Add the lemon juice, remaining olive oil and the parsley, and season well.

5   In a small bowl, mix the crème fraîche with the mustard and season well. Once the veg is cooked, squeeze the garlic from the bulb (it should be soft and golden brown) into the grains and give it a good stir.

6   To assemble, spoon the grains into bowls (or onto a big platter) and top with the roasted veggies. Drizzle with the mustard crème fraîche and finish with the pine nuts and basil leaves. Add a crack of black pepper and a drizzle of olive oil.

 4–8   15 mins   40 mins   Up to 5 days   Up to 1 month

4– Gourds & Legumes

Pumpkin
Squash
Cucumber
Tofu
Chickpeas
Beans

Fresh Cucumber and Apple Salad

Magic happens when you combine cool cucumbers and crunchy apples. This is a perfect side dish for summer picnics and barbecues. It's addictively good and takes just minutes to make.

40g toasted pistachios, crushed
2 tbsp white wine vinegar
1 tsp maple syrup
3 tbsp extra-virgin olive oil
1 large cucumber, halved lengthways, then halved crossways, then cut into 1cm pieces
1 Granny Smith apple, cored and cut into thin half-moon slices (about 3mm thick)
3 small radishes, thinly sliced
115g feta, roughly crumbled
10g fresh basil leaves
2 tbsp freshly torn mint
salt and black pepper

1 Put most of the pistachios (reserving some to garnish) in a food processor. Add the vinegar, maple syrup and oil, and blitz for a few seconds until slightly smooth. Season to taste with salt and black pepper.

2 Combine the remaining salad ingredients in a serving bowl. Pour the pistachio dressing over the top and gently fold through. Sprinkle with the remaining pistachios and season with more salt and black pepper.

Tip This can be prepared 1 day in advance, but leave out the herbs and pistachios until just before serving.

 4   5 mins   Up to 3 days   **GF**

Crisp Cucumber Salsa

With cool cucumber and spicy chilli, this salsa has a surprisingly zingy crunch. It's the perfect accompaniment to any meal, especially my Pulled Mushroom Tacos (page 179), Smoky Lentil and Broccoli Stem Tacos (page 142) or Loaded Nachos (page 19).

2 baby cucumbers, quartered
   lengthways, then thinly sliced
½ red onion, finely chopped
zest and juice of 1 lime
2 tbsp freshly chopped mint
2 tbsp freshly chopped coriander
½ fresh red or green chilli, seeded,
   finely chopped
generous pinch of salt
¼ tsp black pepper

1   In a mixing bowl, combine the cucumbers, red onion, lime juice and zest, mint, coriander and chilli. Season with salt and black pepper and leave for about 10 minutes before serving. This will allow the flavours to marinate and will also remove some of the liquid from the cucumber, providing a less watery crunch.

Tips Make 1 day in advance
if needed; keep for 3 days
in the fridge in a sealed container.

You may want more chilli, or less,
depending on the chilli heat
and how spicy you like it.

 8   15 mins   Up to 3 days   **GF**

Creamy Courgette and Lemon Linguine

This easy pasta dish is a must-make for using up courgettes or summer squash. Flavours of olive oil, shallots and garlic are held together by a lip-smackingly creamy cashew sauce, all lifted by a final squeeze of lemon. Grating courgettes means you can use the entire thing – yes, even the stalk. It all cooks down in the pan since it's mainly water. A fantastic summertime pasta dish that can eaten warm or cold.

2 large courgettes or summer squash
2 tbsp olive oil
1 shallot or ½ small onion, thinly sliced
4 garlic cloves, finely grated
380g linguine or any long pasta
45g raw cashews, soaked in hot water for 20–30 minutes, then rinsed
zest and juice of 1 lemon
30g parmesan, grated, plus more to serve
1 tsp cornflour
2 tbsp extra-virgin olive oil
1 tbsp capers or pitted green olives
3 tbsp chopped fresh basil
3 tbsp chopped fresh mint
salt and black pepper

1 Using the large holes of a box grater, grate the courgettes into a bowl. Use your hands to squeeze out any excess liquid, then place the courgettes on a clean tea towel. Wrap the tea towel around the courgettes and squeeze the remaining liquid out over the sink.

2 Heat the olive oil in a large frying pan over medium heat and cook the shallot for 8–10 minutes, stirring occasionally, until soft. Stir in half of the garlic and cook for 2–3 minutes, until lightly browned. Add the grated courgette and increase the heat to medium–high. Season with salt and black pepper and cook for 3–5 minutes, stirring often, until the courgette begins to soften. Remove from the heat.

3 Meanwhile, bring a large pan of salted water to the boil, add the pasta and cook according to the packet instructions.

4 In a blender, blitz the soaked cashews, the remaining garlic, lemon juice, parmesan, cornflour, extra-virgin olive oil and 4 tablespoons of the pasta cooking water until smooth and creamy; you may need to scrape the sides down halfway through. Season with salt and black pepper.

5 Drain the pasta and immediately transfer to the pan with the courgette, over low heat. Pour half the cashew sauce over the pasta, stirring until the sauce coats the pasta. Toss in the capers, lemon zest, and the basil and mint, reserving a little for a garnish.

6 Serve the pasta in bowls, topped with the remaining sauce, a sprinkle of grated parmesan, and the rest of the basil and mint.

Tip Use gluten-free pasta if you prefer.

 4
 15 mins
 15–20 mins
 Up to 3 days
 Up to 1 month

Roasted Squash and Aubergine with Tahini Yoghurt and Toasted Seeds

In this warm aubergine and squash salad, subtle heat from the harissa dressing is cooled down by creamy tahini yoghurt sauce. It's so versatile: serve as a starter with pitta or flatbreads, or as a main course with rice or through pasta. Go ahead and switch up the type of squash: courgette, pumpkin or butternut squash will all work well. For extra sweetness, feel free to throw in a couple of onions peeled and sliced into wedges too, which will caramelise and soften beautifully in the oven.

530g summer squash, cut into 2cm pieces
1 aubergine, cut into 1cm pieces
4 garlic cloves: 2 lightly crushed, 2 thinly sliced
3 fresh thyme sprigs
zest and juice of 1 lemon
6 tbsp extra-virgin olive oil
1 tbsp tahini
125g yoghurt (I use coconut yoghurt)
2 tbsp pine nuts
2 tbsp sunflower seeds
1 tbsp sesame seeds
1 tsp harissa
2 tbsp freshly chopped dill
salt and black pepper
toasted pitta bread, to serve (optional)

1   Preheat the oven to 170°C/150°C fan/gas 3.

2   In a roasting tin, mix together the squash, aubergine, crushed garlic, thyme sprigs, lemon zest, 3 tablespoons of the olive oil and a generous pinch of salt until everything is coated in the oil. Cook in the oven for about 1½ hours, turning everything over every 30 minutes or so, until the veg is softened and starting to get a little crunchy on the surface. Set aside to cool while you make the rest of the recipe.

3   In a small bowl, whisk the tahini and yoghurt with the lemon juice and a splash of water until smooth and creamy. Season with salt and black pepper.

4   In a frying pan over medium–low heat, toast the pine nuts, sunflower and sesame seeds for about 3 minutes, shaking the pan occasionally, until lightly brown.

5   In another small bowl, whisk together the remaining 3 tablespoons of olive oil, the harissa, thinly sliced garlic and the toasted seed mixture. Season with salt and black pepper.

6   Spread the tahini yoghurt sauce across a serving platter. Top with the veg, the seed mixture and fresh dill. Serve warm, with toasted pitta if you like.

Tip This salad is best served hot.

 4   15 mins   1½ hours   Up to 3 days   Up to 1 month   **GF**

Roast Dinner Tart

This incredible tart has all your favourite elements of a roast dinner. It's the perfect alternative Sunday lunch or festive meal – just don't forget the gravy!

200g beetroot
½ butternut squash
250g carrots
200g parsnips
1 tbsp olive oil
1 x quantity of Best Roast Potatoes (see page 33)
1 x quantity of Buttery Herb Stuffing, page 74
2 tbsp nutritional yeast
1 tsp ground cinnamon
1 tsp grated nutmeg
1 sheet gluten-free puff pastry
oat milk, for brushing
120g Brussels sprouts, halved
6 tbsp cranberry sauce
salt and black pepper
gravy, to serve

Crispy sage
8–10 sage leaves
3 tbsp olive oil

1   Preheat the oven to 240°C/220°C fan/gas 9.

2   Wrap the beetroot in foil and put on one side of a baking tray. Place the squash next to them, cut-side down. Roast for up to 1 hour (depending on their size), until the beetroot are totally soft. If the squash cooks more quickly, remove it from the oven and let the beetroot keep cooking.

3   Slice the carrots and parsnips in half lengthways and put in a roasting tray. Drizzle with olive oil, add a pinch of salt and roast for 30 minutes, until soft and charred.

4   Make the best roast potatoes (according to page 33).

5   Make the stuffing (according to page 74).

6   Scoop the seeds from the cooked squash and set aside (you can rinse them and toast them for a snack). In a blender, blitz the squash with the nutritional yeast, cinnamon and nutmeg. Season well and blitz to a purée.

7   Squeeze the beets from their skins and slice into wedges.

8   Cut the sheet of puff pastry into 4 rectangles. Lightly score a border, 2cm from the edge. Brush with oat milk, then bake for 20–30 minutes until golden and risen; use a spoon to push the middle down.

9   Meanwhile, heat the olive oil in a large frying pan over medium heat, add the sprouts with a pinch of salt and fry for 5 minutes. Add a big splash of water (the steam helps them to cook through) and cook for a further 5 minutes, until tender. Set aside.

10 Make the crispy sage. Heat the oil in a small frying pan over high heat. Once hot, fry the sage for 2 minutes until crispy. Set aside to drain on kitchen paper.

11 Spoon the butternut squash purée onto each pastry rectangle, then crumble over the stuffing. Top with the carrots, parsnips, beetroot and roast potatoes. Scatter over the sprouts, then spoon over a little cranberry sauce. Finish with the crispy sage leaves and serve with lots of gravy.

 4

 30 mins

 1 hour 20 - 30 mins

 Up to 1 week

 Up to 1 month

GF

Curried Pumpkin and Chickpeas

A simple, warm and inviting autumn dish – roasted pumpkin and spiced chickpeas are heaped onto a creamy and tangy yoghurt sauce. It's elevated with toasted coconut flakes, crispy onions and fresh coriander which add texture and extra flavour. Serve with rice and my Fragrant Flatbreads (page 206) to make the ultimate feast!

1 pumpkin (approx. 1kg)

3 tbsp olive oil

2 x 400g tin chickpeas, drained and rinsed (reserve the aquafaba to make my meringues on page 228)

1 tbsp cumin seeds

1–2 tsp chilli powder

200g coconut yoghurt, or another thick yoghurt

2 limes

small handful of fresh coriander, roughly chopped

small handful of fresh mint, roughly chopped

40g crispy onions

40g desiccated coconut flakes, toasted

salt and black pepper

1   Preheat the oven to 220°C/200°C fan/gas 7.

2   Cut the pumpkin in half, remove the seeds, then cut into wedges. Place the wedges, flesh-side up on a large baking sheet. Drizzle with 2 tbsp of the olive oil, season with salt and black pepper and roast for 30 minutes.

3   In another roasting tray, toss the chickpeas with the remaining olive oil, cumin seeds, chilli powder and a generous pinch of salt. Once the pumpkin has been roasting for about 15 minutes, put the tray of chickpeas in the oven and cook for 15 minutes, until the pumpkin and chickpeas are golden brown and crispy.

4   Meanwhile, in a small bowl mix the yoghurt with the zest and juice of 1 lime and half of the fresh herbs. Season with salt and pepper and spread across a large platter.

5   Top with the roasted chickpeas, then the cooked pumpkin wedges. Scatter over the crispy onions, toasted coconut flakes and remaining coriander and mint. Serve with lime wedges.

Tips Try swapping the pumpkin for butternut squash, delicata squash or sweet potato.

The pumpkin seeds can be toasted and enjoyed later as a snack.

4–8   10 mins   30 mins   Up to 5 days   Up to 1 month

Grilled Courgette and Miso-Almond 'Ricotta' Involtini

This is an easy yet impressive dish that is great for entertaining. Strips of grilled courgette are stuffed with creamy almond 'ricotta', rolled up and baked in a flavourful sea of tomato sauce. My almond 'ricotta' is super-easy to make and comes together in minutes. *Photo overleaf*

2 large courgettes (any colour)
2 tbsp olive oil
450g prepared tomato sauce
  (try my Simplest Tomato Sauce,
  page 87)
4 fresh thyme sprigs
salt and black pepper

To serve
chilli flakes
chopped fresh basil
grated parmesan

Almond 'ricotta'
100g sliced almonds, soaked in hot
  water for 20–30 minutes, then rinsed
  and drained
60ml hot water
zest and juice of ½ lemon
2 tsp extra-virgin olive oil
2 tsp white miso
2 tbsp nutritional yeast
2 garlic cloves, finely grated
3 tbsp freshly chopped basil
2 tbsp freshly chopped parsley

1 First, make the almond 'ricotta'. In a high-speed blender, blitz the almonds, hot water, lemon juice and zest, olive oil, miso, nutritional yeast and garlic until smooth but still slightly textured. If it seems a little thick, add a little more hot water. Stir in the basil and parsley, then chill in the fridge.

2 Using a mandoline, sharp knife or Y peeler, slice the courgettes lengthways, including the stems, into thin strips (about 3–5mm thick). Put the strips in a mixing bowl and toss with the olive oil, salt and pepper.

3 Preheat the grill to medium–high. Place a wire rack inside a large roasting tin and arrange the slices of courgette on the rack. Grill for about 5–8 minutes until lightly charred, then flip them over and cook until charred on the other side. Remove from the rack and set aside.

4 Preheat the oven to 190°C/170°C fan/gas 5.

5 Pour the tomato sauce into a 20–22cm ovenproof dish. Set up an assembly line with a cutting board, the grilled courgettes and the almond 'ricotta'. Lay one slice of courgette on the cutting board and place 1 tablespoon of the almond 'ricotta' at the wider end. Carefully and gently roll it up, so that no ricotta squeezes out the sides. Carefully place the rolled courgette in the tomato sauce. Repeat until you have rolled all the courgettes.

6 Place the thyme sprigs on top of the involtini. Cover loosely with foil, to allow steam to escape, and bake for 15–20 minutes, until heated through.

7 Serve hot, sprinkled with chilli flakes, chopped basil grated parmesan.

Tip The almond 'ricotta' can be made 2 days in advance.

 4
 20–30 mins
 25–35 mins
 Up to 3 days
 Up to 1 month
GF

Tofu Butter 'Chicken'

A fan favourite, this is one of my most popular dishes with over 4 million views on my social media channels! Pressing the tofu removes excess water, and coating it with cornflour gives it a thin, crunchy exterior when it's baked until golden in the oven. Paired with a vibrant, creamy sauce, it's winner winner (tofu) chicken dinner!

Tofu
450g extra-firm tofu
2 tbsp cornflour

Sauce
1 large onion, finely chopped
2 tbsp grated fresh ginger
3 garlic cloves, thinly sliced
1 tbsp garam masala
1 tsp cumin seeds or ground cumin
1 tsp coriander seeds
  or ground coriander
½ tsp ground turmeric
½ tsp ground cinnamon
½ tsp chilli powder
pinch of salt and black pepper
3 tbsp tomato purée
3 tbsp butter or olive oil
1 x 400g tin full-fat coconut milk

To serve
toasted coconut flakes
yoghurt (I use coconut yoghurt)
fresh coriander
fluffy basmati rice
Fragrant Flatbreads (page 206)

1 Cut the tofu in half. Wrap each half in a clean tea towel. Stack something heavy on top – such as a weighted pan – and leave for 10–15 minutes to press the liquid from the tofu.

2 Meanwhile, preheat the oven to 200°C/180°C fan/gas 6. Line a baking sheet with baking parchment.

3 Tear the tofu into smaller pieces to resemble pieces of chicken. Place the tofu in a mixing bowl with cornflour and gently toss to coat the tofu pieces. Spread out the tofu pieces on the baking sheet and bake for 20–25 minutes, until the edges start to brown, flipping halfway through.

4 Meanwhile, in a food processor blitz the onion, garlic and ginger to a paste. In a large frying pan over medium heat, toast the spices for 1–2 minutes until fragrant then stir in the paste, and cook for 1 minute. Add the butter, salt and pepper and stir, cooking for 3–4 minutes until the onion mixture is soft. Add the tomato purée and cook for 1 minute. Pour in the coconut milk, stir to combine and simmer for 10 minutes.

5 When the tofu is brown and crispy, take the sauce off the heat and add the baked tofu. Serve with toasted coconut flakes, yoghurt, fresh coriander, fluffy rice and flatbreads.

Tips Some might say that the leftovers are better the next day.

More bulk? Add roasted chickpeas and a handful of leafy greens.

Fun fact It's said that in Delhi in the early 20th century, butter chicken was a way to use up leftover chicken – a perfect fit for a cookbook that's all about cooking the food you already have.

 4
 20 mins
 20–25 mins
 2–3 days
 Up to 3 months
GF

Sticky, Spicy Ginger and Garlic Tofu

This is one of my go-to dishes for midweek meals. The trick here is, once the sauce is poured on the crispy tofu, turn the heat off, stir to coat the tofu and serve immediately. Use the leftover sauce from the pan as an additional glaze for the noodles.

Sauce
60ml soy sauce or tamari
20g coconut sugar or light
  brown sugar
1 tbsp hot sauce
zest and juice of ½ lime
1 tbsp vegetable oil
pinch of salt
¼ tsp black pepper

Spicy tofu
450g firm tofu, lightly crumbled
2 tbsp cornflour
3 tbsp vegetable oil
15g fresh ginger, not peeled, grated
2 garlic cloves, finely chopped

To serve
200g ramen noodles, prepared
  according to packet instructions
1 tbsp sesame seeds, lightly toasted
1–2 spring onions, thinly sliced
2 tbsp freshly chopped coriander
zest of ½ lime
lime wedges

1 First, prepare the sauce: in a mixing bowl, whisk all the ingredients together until smooth and pourable. Set aside.

2 For the spicy tofu, toss the tofu and cornflour in a bowl until evenly coated. Heat the oil in a large non-stick pan over medium heat. Once hot, carefully add the tofu and fry for about 6–8 minutes, stirring often, until crispy and golden brown. Add the ginger and garlic and stir for 1–2 minutes until lightly brown.

3 Carefully pour the sauce over the tofu, remove from the heat, and stir. The sauce should bubble and sizzle.

4 Serve the noodles in bowls, add the spicy tofu, and top with toasted sesame seeds, spring onions, coriander, lime zest and a lime wedge.

Tips Replace the tofu with chickpeas, beans, tempeh or mushrooms.

Use any style of Asian noodle you like: gluten-free works well. Or serve with rice.

I like to use up leftover condiments I have in my fridge – hot sauces, chilli jams, anything pickled – as extra toppings.

 4   10 mins   10 mins   1–2 days   Up to 1 month

Killer Tofu 'Ground Beef'

This is the most popular dish on my social media channels. Use this baked and seasoned tofu in any dishes traditionally prepared with minced beef. It's perfect for nachos (page 19), tacos, shepherd's pie, chilli and so much more. It's super-easy to prepare, the oven does all the hard work for you and, best of all, it's made with just a few basic ingredients you probably already have in your cupboards.

450g extra-firm tofu
3 tbsp soy sauce or tamari
1 tsp garlic powder
1 tsp paprika
1 tsp chilli powder
1 garlic clove, grated
1 tsp cornstarch
1 tsp tomato purée
2 tbsp nutritional yeast
1 tbsp olive oil

1   Preheat the oven to 200°C/180°C fan/gas 6. Line a baking tin with baking parchment.

2   Wrap the tofu in a clean tea towel or kitchen paper and lightly pat for about 2 minutes to remove some of the excess liquid.

3   Add the remaining ingredients (except the oil) to a large bowl and mix together.

4   Into the same mixing bowl, squeeze the pressed tofu between your hands to create a crumbly texture. Mix well to coat the tofu thoroughly.

5   Tip the tofu into the baking tin and spread out into one even layer. Drizzle the oil over the tofu and bake for 20 minutes, tossing halfway through so it crisps up all over.

 4
 5 mins

 20 mins
 2–3 days
Up to 3 months

Chickpea 'Tuna' Salad

I'm happy to admit that I'm a tiny bit competitive, and so if my wife makes something in the kitchen, I'll usually try to make it better! This recipe is based on a lunch she cooked for us one day – but it's my improved version! Mashed chickpeas are given a distinctly fish-like flavour from the nori, and it has loads of texture from all the crunchy veg and seeds. It's a great protein-packed topping for baked potatoes or to use in sandwiches.

1 x 400g tin chickpeas, drained and rinsed (reserve aquafaba for another recipe)
3 tbsp mayo
zest and juice of 1 lemon
½ red onion, finely chopped
1 red pepper, seeded and diced
2 celery sticks, thinly sliced, including the leaves
2 tbsp capers
3 tbsp toasted sunflower or pumpkin seeds
2 tbsp freshly chopped dill
1 nori sheet, thinly sliced or flaked
pinch of salt
¼ tsp black pepper

1 Put the chickpeas in a mixing bowl and crush, using the back of a fork or a potato masher, until the chickpeas are roughly mashed.

2 Add the mayo, lemon juice and zest, red onion, red pepper, celery, capers, toasted seeds, dill, nori, salt and black pepper. Mix to your desired consistency.

3 Serve chilled or at room temperature.

Tips Serve on toasted bread, in a wrap or sandwich, or on a baked potato.

For a gluten-free version, serve on romaine lettuce leaves with cherry tomatoes.

Optional extras: add sweetcorn, peas, edamame, grated carrot, chopped cherry tomatoes.

 4 10 mins 1–2 days Up to 1 month **GF**

Crispy Tofu Burger

Coated in breadcrumbs and shallow-fried until golden brown, this almost exactly resembles the textures of a crispy fish burger. Pile into a ciabatta bun with all your favourite toppings – and be generous with the burger sauce.

100g flour
160ml oat milk
1 tsp smoked paprika
50g panko breadcrumbs
  or home-made breadcrumbs
2 tbsp sesame seeds
280g firm tofu, sliced horizontally
  into 4 rectangles, around 2cm thick
vegetable oil, for frying

Burger sauce
4 tbsp ketchup
4 tbsp mayo
1 tbsp Dijon mustard
  or American mustard
juice of ½ lemon

To serve
4 ciabatta rolls
½ cucumber, cut into 1cm-thick slices
1–2 tomatoes, depending on their size,
  cut into 1cm-thick slices
1 iceberg lettuce, shredded

1 In a small bowl, make the burger sauce by combining everything together. Keep the sauce and the prepared veg to serve in the fridge to keep cool.

2 In a bowl, whisk the flour, oat milk and smoked paprika to make a thick batter. Combine the breadcrumbs and sesame seeds in a separate shallow bowl. Dip each of the tofu rectangles first in the batter, then dredge in the sesame breadcrumbs to coat all over.

3 Pour the vegetable oil ½cm up the sides of heavy-based frying pan over medium–high heat. Once the oil is shimmering – after 2–3 minutes – do a 'sizzle check' by dropping a few breadcrumbs into the oil. If they sizzle, it's ready to go! Gently lower the breaded tofu into the oil and cook for 2–3 minutes on each side, until golden and crispy. Remove with a slotted spoon and drain on a wire rack or plate lined with kitchen paper. You may need to do this in 2 batches.

4 Slice the ciabatta rolls in half, lightly toast and slather one side with the burger sauce. Layer up the crispy tofu, with slices of cucumber and tomato and the shredded lettuce. Eat ASAP.

Tip Best served hot!

 4 15 mins 15 mins Up to 1 month

Peas and Beans Fritters

These super-green fritters are so quick and easy to make and are one of my favourite ways to enjoy peas and beans. Serve as an appetiser or side, or make them smaller for tasty canapés.

400g frozen peas
1 x 400g tin white beans, such as cannellini or butter beans, drained and rinsed
5 tbsp gram flour
2 garlic cloves, finely chopped
2 spring onions, thinly sliced
zest and juice of 1 lemon, plus more to serve (optional)
2 tbsp freshly chopped mint
2 tbsp freshly chopped parsley
2 tbsp freshly chopped dill
olive oil or vegetable oil, for frying
salt and black pepper
yoghurt (I use coconut or soy), to serve

1 Put the frozen peas in a large bowl, cover with boiling water and leave for about 1 minute to defrost. Drain and set aside.

2 In a food processor, pulse the white beans with half of the peas to a roughly mashed texture, then tip back into the bowl with the remaining peas. Add the gram flour, garlic, spring onions, lemon juice and zest, and the herbs (reserving a few to garnish if you wish). Season with a generous pinch of salt and black pepper and mix well.

3 Place a large non-stick frying pan over medium heat and pour in enough oil to cover the base. Add a few tablespoons of the mixture to make each fritter and fry for about 3 minutes on each side, carefully flipping, until the edges are crispy. Remove with a slotted spoon and drain on a wire rack or plate lined with kitchen paper. You may need to do this in 2 batches.

4 Serve the fritters warm or at room temperature, with yoghurt; if you wish, sprinkle with lemon juice and zest and fresh herbs.

Tip Any leftovers are great for breakfast or lunch the next day with a dollop of yoghurt or sour cream(see page 19 for Sour Cream).

 6   10 mins   20 mins   Up to 3 days   Up to 1 month GF

Smoked Pea Carbonara

I'm a bit obsessed with this dish! Tofu is used in two ways: for the crispy 'pancetta' and to produce the luxurious creamy sauce. It's all brought together with pops of colour and sweetness from the peas.

100g frozen peas
400g spaghetti
200g smoked extra-firm tofu, pressed to remove water, then cut into small cubes
1 tbsp cornstarch
½ tsp smoked paprika
2 tbsp olive oil
2 garlic cloves, minced
parmesan, to serve

The sauce
300g silken tofu
4 tbsp oat milk
1 tsp Dijon mustard
zest and juice of 1 lemon
1 tbsp nutritional yeast
1 tbsp white miso paste
⅛ tsp black pepper

1 Bring a large pan of salted water to the boil. As it's coming to the boil, make the sauce by blitzing all the ingredients in a high-speed blender and set aside.

2 Tip the peas into a heatproof bowl, cover with boiling water, leave for 2 minutes, then drain and set aside.

3 Add the spaghetti to the pan of boiling water and cook for 1 minute less than packet instructions.

4 While the spaghetti cooks, in a mixing bowl lightly toss the cubed tofu, cornstarch and smoked paprika until evenly coated. Heat the olive oil in a large frying pan over high heat and once warm, fry the cubed smoked tofu, stirring occasionally, for 8–10 minutes until crispy and brown. Add the garlic and cook for 30 seconds.

5 When the pasta is almost ready, pour the sauce into the frying pan with the tofu, stirring frequently, and cook until bubbling. Use tongs to slosh the pasta from the saucepan into the large frying pan with the sauce. Add the peas and toss everything well.

6 Serve in bowls, topped with black pepper and parmesan.

Tip Make your own smoked tofu by marinating a block of tofu with 1 tablespoon soy sauce or tamari, 2 teaspoons liquid smoke, 1 teaspoon smoked paprika and 1 teaspoon maple syrup overnight in a small container. Make sure that the tofu is well coated in the sauce.

 4
 10 mins
 15 mins
 Up to 5 days
 Up to 1 month

Lentil Pappa Pomodoro

This dish came about as a result of a happy accident in my kitchen. I had some leftover lentil ragù and I didn't want to cook pasta, so I added some bread to it – and hey presto! Satisfying, grounded and delicious, the bread adds extra bulk to the rich tomato soup.

1 tbsp olive oil, plus more to drizzle
1 onion, finely chopped
2 cloves garlic, finely sliced
1 tsp dried oregano
½ tsp fennel seeds
200g cooked Puy lentils
2 tbsp tomato purée
2 x 400g tins plum tomatoes
500ml veg stock
pinch of sugar (optional)
200g crusty bread, torn
salt and black pepper
basil leaves, to serve

1   Heat the olive oil in a saucepan over medium heat. Add the onion and a big pinch of salt and fry, stirring often, for 5–8 minutes, until softened. Add the garlic, oregano, fennel seeds and lentils, and cook for 2 minutes. Stir in the tomato purée and cook for a further 1–2 minutes. Add the tomatoes and stock, stirring to combine. Turn the heat down to a simmer and cook for 20–25 minutes, until slightly thickened and fragrant. Taste and season with salt and pepper and pinch of sugar if it needs it.

2   Preheat the oven to 200°C/180°C fan/gas 6.

3   While the sauce is cooking, put the torn crusty bread on a baking sheet, drizzle with 2 teaspoons of olive oil and toss together. Bake for 5–7 minutes, until lightly crispy and golden brown.

4   Add the crusty bread to the tomato mixture and cook for 3–5 minutes, stirring often. If it looks a little thick, add a splash of water to help loosen it. Spoon into bowls, drizzle with olive oil and scatter with basil leaves. Finish with a crack of black pepper.

Tip   You can swap out the lentils for chickpeas.

 6
 5 mins
 30–45 mins
 Up to 5 days
 Up to 1 month

Gourds & Legumes

No-bake Pumpkin Pie in a Jar

What could be better than getting a mini pumpkin pie in a jar all to yourself?! These individual, no-'oven'-required, make-ahead desserts are made up of layers of crunchy pecan crust, spiced pumpkin and silky coconut cream. This recipe makes four, but it easily doubles, triples or quadruples. You can make them ahead and leave in the fridge to chill.

Coconut cream
180g full-fat coconut cream,
   at room temperature
3 tbsp cream cheese
½ tsp vanilla extract
1 tbsp maple syrup

Pecan crust
100g pecans
60g Medjool dates, pits removed
50g almond flour
2 tsp light brown sugar
1 tsp ground cinnamon
generous pinch of salt

Pumpkin filling
350g cooked pumpkin
   or butternut squash
20g full-fat coconut cream
30g maple syrup
2 tbsp icing sugar
1 tsp ground cinnamon
½ tsp ground nutmeg
½ tsp ground ginger
pinch of salt

1   First, make the coconut cream by whisking all the ingredients together until light and fluffy, then chill for 30 minutes.

2   To make the pecan crust, pulse the ingredients in a food processor to a light crumble consistency, then tip into a bowl.

3   To make the pumpkin filling, blend the ingredients in a food processor until smooth and creamy.

4   To assemble, you will need 4 small glass jars. Add a thin layer of the pecan crust to each jar, then a layer of the pumpkin filling and then the coconut cream. Repeat until you reach the top of the jar. Finish with a light dusting of the pecan crust.

5   Chill for at least 1–2 hours or overnight before serving.

 4   10 mins   Up to 7 days   Up to 1 month   **GF**

5– Leafy Greens & Cruciferous

Cauliflower
Broccoli
Herbs

Smoky Lentil and Broccoli Stem Tacos

Meat-eaters and vegans alike will enjoy this budget-friendly take on tacos. A handful of surprisingly simple ingredients lends big flavours and 'meaty' textures to the smoky lentil and broccoli stem taco filling.

2 tbsp olive oil
½ red onion, thinly sliced
1 large broccoli stem, grated
1 x 400g tin green lentils, drained and rinsed
2 garlic cloves, finely chopped
4 sundried tomatoes, roughly chopped
1 tbsp tomato purée
1 tbsp soy sauce or tamari
1 tsp smoked paprika
1 tsp ground cumin
1 tbsp nutritional yeast
¼ tsp black pepper

To serve
8–12 corn or flour tortillas, warmed
Crisp Cucumber Salsa (page 114)
freshly chopped coriander and basil
lime wedges

1 Heat the oil in a large frying pan over medium heat and cook the onion for 3–5 minutes, stirring occasionally, until soft. Add the grated broccoli stem, lentils, garlic and sundried tomatoes and cook for 2–3 minutes, stirring occasionally.

2 Add all the remaining ingredients and cook for about 3 minutes, stirring frequently, until the mixture thickens and begins to stick to the pan. Stir in 1–2 tablespoons of water for the last minute of cooking. Remove from the heat and cover with a lid while you warm the tortillas.

3 To serve, spoon the lentil and broccoli stem mixture onto warm tortillas and top with Cucumber Salsa, fresh coriander and basil, with lime wedges on the side.

Tips Super-versatile: sub for the Killer Tofu 'Ground Beef' in the Loaded Nachos on page 19, use in a chilli, burritos and rice bowls.

If gluten is an issue for you, ensure you use tamari, a gluten-free version of soy sauce, and gluten-free corn tortillas.

 4
 10 mins
 10–15 mins
 Up to 3 days
 Up to 1 month

Broccoli Stem Fried Rice

Did you know that broccoli plants can grow several feet high? What are we doing with all those stems?! Broccoli stems have a fantastic, subtly sweet flavour. You can eat them raw, sliced in a salad, or grate them into this quick and tasty midweek sir-fry, which has become one of my favourite ways to use up leftover broccoli stems.

180ml water or veg stock
135g white or brown rice, rinsed
1 tbsp olive oil
1 thumb-sized piece of ginger, finely grated
4 garlic cloves, thinly sliced
240g shiitake mushrooms, sliced if large
1 large broccoli stem, grated
1 tbsp butter
2 tbsp soy sauce or tamari
1 tsp maple syrup
zest and juice of ½ lemon

To serve
20–30g red cabbage, thinly shredded
½ carrot, cut into thin matchsticks
2 tbsp finely chopped fresh coriander
2 tbsp finely chopped fresh chives
1–2 tbsp toasted sesame seeds
½ tsp chilli flakes

1 In a pan, bring the water to the boil. Add the rice, gently stir, reduce the heat and simmer, uncovered, for 10–15 minutes or until the rice is cooked. (Brown rice will take 20–30 minutes to cook, and you may need to top up the pan with more boiling water.) Drain and set aside.

2 Meanwhile, add the oil to a non-stick frying pan over medium heat, stir in the ginger and garlic and cook for 1 minute, until fragrant. Add the mushrooms and cook for 3–5 minutes, stirring occasionally, until the mushrooms are soft. Add the grated broccoli stem and cook for another 3–5 minutes, stirring often, until the mixture begins to stick to the pan.

3 Using a wooden spoon, push the veg to one side of the pan and melt the butter, then add the cooked rice and stir to combine everything. Add the soy sauce, maple syrup and lemon juice and stir again, then leave to cook for 3–5 minutes without stirring, until the rice is slightly charred and begins to stick to the pan.

4 Serve the fried rice on a serving plate; top with shredded cabbage and carrot, chopped herbs, toasted sesame seeds, chilli flakes and lemon zest.

Tips Super-versatile: add chopped leftover veggies from your fridge.

Add protein: crispy tofu, roasted chickpeas or imitation 'meat'.

Use day-old cooked rice to make fried rice (another great way to waste less food) - but in this case, don't freeze.

If gluten is an issue for you, ensure you use tamari, a gluten-free version of soy sauce.

 4 15 mins 15–20 mins 1 day Up to 1 month

Sticky Broccoli and Crispy Tofu

Crispy tofu is served with broccoli tossed in a sweet, spicy glaze. The key to crispy tofu is ensuring it's as dry as possible before it goes into the hot oil. You don't need takeaway when you can make something more delicious in less time.

Crispy tofu
280g extra-firm tofu
2 tbsp cornflour
4 tbsp vegetable oil
salt and black pepper

Glazed broccoli
225–250g broccoli, cut into florets,
   stems sliced lengthways
zest and juice of 1 lime
2 tsp soy sauce or tamari
2 tsp maple syrup or brown sugar
½ tsp chilli flakes

To serve
rice or noodles
1–2 tbsp crushed toasted peanuts

1   Wrap the tofu in a clean tea towel, cover with a weighted pan and leave for 15–20 minutes. Blot the tofu dry, then cut into cubes.

2   In a large mixing bowl, toss the tofu with the cornflour until evenly coated.

3   Heat the oil in a large non-stick frying pan over medium–high heat. Once hot, carefully add the tofu – without overcrowding the pan – and fry, undisturbed, for 2–3 minutes until goldenbrown and crispy on one side. Cook for a further 5–7 minutes, stirring occasionally, to fry all sides. Remove from the heat and add a pinch of salt and black pepper.

4   Meanwhile, steam or blanch the broccoli in boiling water for about 3–4 minutes until tender. Drain the broccoli and add to a non-stick frying pan over medium heat with the lime juice, soy sauce, maple syrup and chilli flakes. Cook for 2 minutes, stirring often, until the broccoli is glazed and sticky.

5   Serve the sticky broccoli over fluffy rice or noodles, topped with the crispy tofu, crushed peanuts and lime zest.

Tips Make the broccoli sauce in advance or make more to freeze.

Swap broccoli for cauliflower or kale, carrots, sweet potatoes, sugar snap peas.

 2   10 mins   10 mins   Up to 3 days   Up to 1 month

Cauliflower Ragù

Cauliflower is one of my favourite ingredients to work with as it takes on flavours incredibly well and is so adaptable – it can be smooth and creamy or crunchy and crisp! It holds its texture perfectly in this rich and hearty ragù.

1 large cauliflower
2 tbsp olive oil
2 tbsp butter
1 onion, finely diced
3 garlic cloves, minced
1 tbsp dried oregano
2–3 sprigs of fresh rosemary, leaves
　picked and finely chopped
10 tbsp tomato purée
100ml red wine
400g pappardelle
salt and black pepper

To serve
grated parmesan
a few fresh basil leaves

1 In a food processor, pulse the entire cauliflower in batches, including the core and leaves, until it resembles a rice texture. Tip into a bowl and set aside.

2 Heat the olive oil and butter in a large saucepan or Dutch oven over medium heat. Fry the onion with a generous pinch of salt and black pepper for 5 minutes, until soft. Add the garlic, dried oregano and rosemary leaves, and cook for 1 minute. Add the tomato purée and cook, stirring well, for 2 minutes.

3 Add the riced cauliflower to the pan and stir until combined. Pour in the red wine and cook for 3–5 minutes, until the wine evaporates. Reduce the heat to low while you cook the pasta.

4 Cook the pappardelle in a large saucepan of salted boiling water according to the packet instructions. When the pasta is cooked, use tongs to slosh the pasta from the water into the saucepan with the sauce, and toss together. Use a little of the pasta cooking liquid if you need to loosen the sauce. Swirl into bowls, top with parmesan and basil leaves, and serve.

 8

 5 mins

 20–25 mins

 Up to 5 days

 Up to 1 month

Spicy Baked Cauliflower Wings

These sticky and spicy cauliflower 'wings' are a BIG fan favourite! Loaded with flavour, these are the best match-day snack or Friday night treat. Without the spicy hot sauce, they're crispy and crunchy on the outside and soft on the inside. With the sauce, they're a knockout!

1 large cauliflower, cut into 3–5cm florets, core sliced, leaves separated

Batter
35g gram flour or plain flour
1 tsp ground turmeric
2 tsp chilli powder
½ tsp black pepper
125ml oat milk

Breadcrumb mix
80g dried breadcrumbs (home-made or panko)
2 tsp smoked paprika
½ tsp black pepper
generous pinch of salt

Quick buffalo sauce
2 tbsp hot sauce
3 tbsp tomato ketchup
2 tbsp butter
2 tbsp oat milk
1 tbsp maple syrup
1 tbsp cornflour
2 tsp water

To serve
1 tbsp toasted sesame seeds
1–2 spring onions, thinly sliced
1–2 tbsp snipped fresh chives

1 Preheat the oven to 180°C/160°C fan/gas 4. Line a baking tin with baking parchment.

2 In a mixing bowl, combine all the batter ingredients and whisk until the mixture is smooth and slightly thick.

3 In a separate bowl, combine the breadcrumb mix.

4 Add the cauliflower pieces and leaves to the batter and mix to coat evenly. Next, place the cauliflower in the breadcrumb mix and coat evenly. Place the cauliflower on the lined baking tin and bake for 18–20 minutes, flipping halfway through, until the cauliflower is golden brown and crispy.

5 Meanwhile, make the buffalo sauce. In a pan over medium–low heat, stir together the hot sauce, ketchup, butter, oat milk and maple syrup as it comes to a simmer, then cook for 2–3 minutes. In a small bowl, whisk together the cornflour and water until well combined. Reduce the heat under the pan and stir in the cornflour mixture for about 2 minutes, until smooth and silky. Remove from the heat and set aside.

6 Put the baked cauliflower in a large mixing bowl, add a few spoonfuls of the buffalo sauce and mix to coat evenly.

7 Serve hot, with a sprinkle of sesame seeds, spring onions and chives.

  4–8
 15 mins
  20 mins
Up to 1 month

Tips As a snack or side dish on their own, they're a 10/10 – or serve with sticks of raw veg (carrots, celery) or in a sandwich roll or tortilla.

As a main dish for 4, serve with rice bowls, noodles or tacos.

Swap cauliflower for broccoli.

Any leftovers are not fridge friendly as they will go soft and mushy.

The amount of batter and breadcrumbs will vary depending on the size of the cauliflower. If you need more batter, add a little more flour and milk.

Use gram flour (chickpea flour) for a gluten-free batter.

Air-fryer friendly.

Sticky Cauliflower Wedges with Herby and Crunchy Rice

Sticky roasted cauliflower is the hero in this fun crowd-pleaser of a dish. It has an incredible combination of textures and flavours: wild rice adds bite, which goes with the fresh pop of pomegranate seeds and crunch of pistachios, which contrasts with the soft, caramelised cauliflower and fresh herbs. Every mouthful is an adventure! It's a dish to make when you want to show off.

2 cauliflowers (or 1 large)
300g wild rice
25g fresh parsley, roughly chopped
25g fresh mint, roughly chopped
1 small pomegranate, seeds removed (approx. 200g seeds)
zest of 1 lemon
2 tbsp olive oil
2 tsp Dijon mustard
60g roasted pistachios, roughly chopped
2 tbsp tahini
salt and black pepper
2 tbsp sesame seeds, to serve

The glaze
2 tbsp pomegranate molasses, plus more to drizzle (optional)
1 tbsp maple syrup
2 tbsp olive oil
2 tsp ground coriander
1 tbsp harissa paste
juice of 1 lemon

1   Preheat the oven to 220°C/200°C fan/gas 7.

2   In a small bowl, mix together the ingredients for the glaze.

3   Cut the cauliflower into 4 large wedges through the root; you can leave the leaves on. Place the wedges on a baking tray and use a brush to coat with the glaze. Season with salt and roast for 25 minutes, until charred and soft. Turn the cauliflower over and cook for a further 10 minutes.

4   Meanwhile, rinse the rice under cold running water until the water runs clear. Drain, then tip into a saucepan and cover with 600ml cold water. Bring to the boil, then turn down to a simmer, cover with a lid and cook for 15 minutes, until tender. Remove from the heat and leave with the lid on to steam for 5 more minutes.

5   Stir through most of the herbs, the pomegranate seeds, zest of the lemon, the olive oil and the mustard. Fold through most of the pistachios. Season well and set aside.

6   Put the tahini and a splash of water or lemon juice in a clean jam jar, seal the lid and shake until smooth and drizzleable.

7   Spoon the cooked rice onto a large platter, topped with the charred cauliflower. Drizzle over the tahini, scatter with the reserved herbs and pistachios and the sesame seeds. Drizzle with a little extra pomegranate molasses if you like!

Tip You can use broccoli or Romanesco instead of the cauliflower.

 4
 20 mins
 35 mins
 1–3 days
 Up to 1 month

Roasted Cauliflower That's Anything But Boring

Cauliflower gets a bad rep for being bland – but I see it more as a blank canvas! It's an incredibly versatile ingredient that can take on flavours well. Coating it in cornstarch before roasting produces a lovely crunchy coating, while the creamy mustard-maple-tahini sauce brings a sweet warmth. Seeds and chives add a pop of colour and extra crunch, making this dish definitely not boring! A great main dish for two, either on its own or with tacos, pasta or rice dishes, or perfect as a side dish for four.

1 large cauliflower, separate florets,
   leaves and core
2 tbsp olive oil
3 tbsp cornflour
generous pinch of salt
¼ tsp black pepper

Tahini mustard lemon sauce
1 tbsp tahini
2 tsp Dijon mustard
juice of ½ lemon
1 tsp maple syrup

To serve
2 tsp toasted sesame seeds
snipped fresh chives

1 Preheat the oven to 200°C/180°C fan/gas 6. Line a large baking sheet with baking parchment.

2 Put the cauliflower florets and leaves in a large mixing bowl, slice the core and add that too, then add the olive oil and toss until evenly coated. Sprinkle with the cornflour, salt and black pepper and mix again.

3 Spread the cauliflower mixture on the lined baking sheet and roast for 17–20 minutes, until the cauliflower is just tender, a deep golden colour and beginning to brown at the edges.

4 Meanwhile, put all the sauce ingredients into a small jar or bowl, close the lid and shake vigorously, or whisk until smooth.

5 Tip the roasted cauliflower back into the mixing bowl. Drizzle over the tahini mustard lemon sauce and mix well.

6 Serve hot, on a large platter or individual plates or bowls. Sprinkle with toasted sesame seeds and chives.

Tips Don't overcrowd the baking sheet.

Swap cauliflower for broccoli.

Make extra sauce for a rainy day: it will keep for up to 5 days in the fridge

 2–4   10 mins   20 mins Up to 3 days   Up to 1 month GF

Stems and Herbs Pesto

A high percentage of our food waste comes from the offcuts of veg and herbs - but there's so much flavour and goodness in those odds and ends. I've used broccoli stems here, but any green stalks - even those tough kale ribs - would work. Throw them all into this incredible, vibrant pesto and spread it in a sandwich or toastie (see page 93), toss through potato salads or any type of pasta - or use it instead of the tomato purée in my Roast Potatoes on page 33.

1–2 broccoli stems, roughly chopped
4 garlic cloves, not peeled
2 tbsp extra-virgin olive oil, plus more
  for drizzling
200g malfade or fusilli pasta
2–3 large handfuls of mixed greens
  and soft herbs from the fridge,
  reserve some herbs for garnish
30g toasted sunflower or pumpkin
  seeds, plus more to serve
3 tbsp nutritional yeast
1 tbsp grated parmesan, plus more
  to serve
zest and juice of 1 lemon
1 tbsp butter

1 Preheat the oven to 180°C/160°C fan/gas 4. Line a baking tin with baking parchment.

2 Put the broccoli stems and garlic in the baking tin and roast for 10–12 minutes, until lightly charred and the broccoli stem is soft. Set aside to cool for 5 minutes before blending.

3 Meanwhile, bring a large pan of salted water to the boil, add the pasta and cook until al dente. Drain, reserving 50ml of the pasta cooking water.

4 Into a food processor or blender, squeeze the garlic from its skin and blend with the broccoli stems, mixed greens and herbs, toasted seeds, nutritional yeast, parmesan and lemon juice. With the motor running, stream in the extra-virgin olive oil and the reserved pasta water until the pesto is very smooth.

5 Return the drained pasta to its pan over low heat and gently stir in the butter. Add the pesto and lemon zest and stir to coat the pasta. Serve topped with more toasted seeds, parmesan and mixed herbs.

Tips Leftover spinach, carrot tops or celery leaves can all be included in place of herbs.

Store in a clean jar and pour in a 1cm layer of olive oil to preserve for up to 2 weeks.

Use gluten-free pasta if you prefer.

 2

 10 mins

 15 mins

 3–4 days

 Up to 1 month

Mighty Green Quiche

I know tofu can be a bit unpopular, but I love how incredibly versatile it is! Blitzed until smooth it perfectly replicates the rich, creamy egg mixture of a classic quiche. With spinach, kale and feta folded through, you can cut a slice of this any time – for breakfast, lunch or dinner – and leftovers taste even better the next day.

1 sheet shortcrust pastry
1 tbsp olive oil
100g spinach, roughly chopped
100g kale, leaves stripped from stems
  and roughly chopped
2 garlic cloves
1 tsp fennel seeds
1 tsp cumin seeds
280g extra-firm tofu
3–4 tbsp oat milk
1 tsp cornstarch
30g feta
salt and black pepper

1   Line a 20cm tart case with the pastry, gently pressing it into the sides. Chill in the fridge for 20 minutes.

2   Preheat the oven to 180°C/160°C fan/gas 4.

3   While the pastry case is chilling, heat the olive oil in a large frying pan over medium heat. Cook the spinach and kale for 4–5 minutes, until wilted and dark green. Crush the garlic into the pan and add the fennel, cumin seeds and a pinch of salt and black pepper. Stirring often, cook for 2 minutes, then remove from the heat.

4   Scrunch up a piece of baking paper, un-scrunch it, then use it to line the pastry tart case. Fill with baking beans or rice, then blind bake for 10–15 minutes. Remove the beans or rice, and cook for a further 5 minutes, until the pastry is pale and dry.

5   In a food processor or blender, blitz the tofu, oat milk and cornstarch until smooth. Add the wilted greens mixture and blend again until well combined.

6   Tip the green mixture into the case, then sprinkle the feta chunks on top. Bake for 30 minutes, until the filling is cooked through and the pastry is golden brown and cooked through. Set aside to cool for at least 15 minutes before serving.

Tip Can be made in advance, keep chilled. Want a slightly warmer quiche? Heat in the oven at 150°C/130°C fan/gas 2 for 5 minutes.

 4   50 mins–1 hour   Up to 5 days   Up to 1 month

Easy Spinach and Chickpea Curry

This curry is a weeknight must-make: quicker and much more satisfying than ordering and waiting for a takeaway. It's perfectly complemented with my easy Fragrant Flatbreads (page 206).

2 tbsp vegetable oil
1 onion, chopped
4 garlic cloves, finely chopped
20g fresh ginger, not peeled, grated
½ tsp brown mustard seeds
1 tsp cumin seeds or ground cumin
1 tbsp madras curry powder
120g carrot, not peeled,
  roughly chopped
1 x 400g tin chickpeas, drained
  and rinsed
100g cherry tomatoes, halved
½ tsp salt
¼ tsp black pepper
60g spinach (fresh or frozen)
1 x 400g tin full-fat coconut milk

To serve
basmati rice
poppadoms
chopped fresh coriander and mint
yoghurt
Pickled Red Onion (page 267)
lime wedges

1 Heat the oil in a non-stick frying pan over medium heat and fry the onion for 5 minutes, until soft. Add the garlic, ginger, mustard seeds, cumin and curry powder and cook for 2 minutes, stirring often, until fragrant.

2 Add the carrot, chickpeas and tomatoes and cook for 8 minutes, until soft. Season with the salt and pepper.

3 Meanwhile, using a hand blender, blitz the spinach and coconut milk until smooth.

4 Pour the green mixture into the frying pan, bring to the boil and simmer over low heat for 10 minutes, stirring occasionally. Remove from the heat and leave to cool for a few minutes before serving.

5 Serve with fluffy basmati rice, poppadoms, fresh coriander and mint, a dollop of yoghurt, pickled red onion and lime wedges.

 4   10 mins   25 mins   Up to 3 days   Up to 1 month   **GF**

Fridge Greens Fusilli

Go to your fridge and pull out those unused greens and get them involved in this warm, delicious, super-green pasta dish. You don't need to be meat-free to love how simple and delicious this is – that's why it's a fan favourite.

3 garlic cloves, not peeled
340g fusilli or pasta shells
280g greens (e.g. rocket, spinach and/or kale, fresh or frozen, including the stems)
handful of fresh basil, including the stems
handful of fresh parsley, including the stems
2 tbsp extra-virgin olive oil
30g parmesan, grated, plus more to serve
2 tbsp nutritional yeast
½ tsp salt
¼ tsp black pepper

1 Preheat the oven to 200°C/180°C fan/gas 6. Put the garlic on a baking sheet and bake for 8 minutes until soft and lightly brown. Remove the skins; set aside.

2 Meanwhile, bring a large pan of salted water to the boil, add the pasta and cook according to the packet instructions. For the last 2 minutes of cooking the pasta, add the greens to the boiling water and cook until soft.

3 Using tongs, carefully lift out the veg and transfer to a blender. Add the roasted garlic, the herbs, olive oil, parmesan, nutritional yeast, salt and black pepper. Blend until super-smooth and creamy.

4 Drain the pasta, reserving a few tablespoons of the cooking water.

5 Return the pasta to its pan along with the bright green sauce. If needed, loosen with a splash of the reserved cooking water, and stir to combine.

6 Serve the pasta in bowls, sprinkled with more grated parmesan.

Tip Use gluten-free pasta if you prefer.

 4
 10 mins
 15 mins
 2–3 days
 Up to 1 month

Greens and Feta Tarte Soleil

Inspired by the flavours of a Greek spanakopita, this pastry centrepiece takes a little time to pull together – but is so worth it. You can use any combination of leafy greens.

280g mixed leafy greens, roughly chopped (e.g. spinach, kale, rocket, lettuce, pak choi)
2 tbsp freshly chopped dill
2 tbsp freshly chopped mint
3 spring onions, thinly sliced
zest of 1 lemon
60g feta, crumbled
30g walnuts, roughly chopped
2 garlic cloves, grated
2 sheets puff pastry
plain flour, for dusting
2 tbsp olive oil
1 tbsp milk
salt and black pepper

1   In a large mixing bowl, combine the leafy greens, herbs, spring onions, lemon zest, feta, walnuts, garlic, a generous pinch of salt and ¼ teaspoon black pepper and stir well to combine until it's a thick, spreadable paste. Set aside.

2   Place one of the pastry sheets on a lightly floured work surface (or still on its paper) and dust lightly with flour on both sides to keep it from sticking. If necessary, roll it out, but don't make it too thin. Place a plate, around 22cm diameter, on top of the pastry and use a knife to cut around it. (Wrap and chill the leftover pastry to use in another recipe.) Lift the pastry circle onto a baking sheet, cover with a clean dry tea towel and chill. Repeat with the second sheet of pastry and chill them both for about 10 minutes.

3   Spoon the filling onto one of the pastry circles, leaving a 1cm border all the way round. Mix the olive oil and milk together and brush around the edge of the pastry. Cover with the second pastry circle, and use your fingers to gently press and seal the two pieces of pastry together.

4   Now you're going to create the soleil part of your tart! Gently press a small glass (about 5cm diameter) in the middle of the pastry. Using a large sharp knife, cut the pastry into quarters – but stop at the indent the glass made in the middle. Then cut each quarter into quarters, to make 16 'sun rays'. Chill for 10–15 minutes.

5   Gently lift up one 'sun ray' and twist it over 3 times. Bring the outer edge of the pastry roughly back to where it started. Repeat all around your sun. Chill again for 10–15 minutes.

6   Meanwhile, preheat the oven to 200°C/180°C fan/gas 6.

7   Brush the pastry with the remaining olive oil and milk wash, sprinkle with salt and black pepper and bake for about 35 minutes, until the pastry is a deep golden brown. Serve hot or at room temperature.

Tips If at any point the pastry becomes too soft, place it in the fridge for 10 minutes.

To reheat from frozen, bake at 150°C/130°C fan/gas 2 for 10-15 minutes until the pastry is crispy again.

 4   30 mins   35 mins   1 day   Up to 1 month

Baking Sheet Pesto Pizza

A square of pizza is perfect for a snack, or serve two or three squares for a main meal for four. The tomato and cheese base is topped with a tasty kale pesto and handfuls of rocket and herbs. Depending on how far in advance you want to make this, you can choose how long to ferment the dough. *Photo overleaf*

150ml lukewarm water
1½ tsp dried active yeast,
 or 1 tsp instant (fast-action) yeast
200g plain flour, plus more for dusting
50g wholemeal flour or rye flour
generous pinch of salt
1 tsp sugar
2 tbsp extra-virgin olive oil, plus more
 for drizzling
200–250g prepared tomato sauce
 (try my Simplest Tomato Sauce,
 page 00)
75g parmesan cheese, grated,
 plus more to serve

Kale pesto
200g kale, leaves stripped from stems
 and roughly chopped
60g mixed nuts or seeds, toasted
3 tbsp extra-virgin olive oil
2 tbsp nutritional yeast
zest and juice of 1 lemon
½ tsp salt
¼ tsp black pepper

To serve
100g fresh rocket
4 tbsp freshly chopped herbs
 (e.g. basil, dill, parsley)
2 tsp balsamic vinegar
½ tsp chilli flakes

Tips If using instant (fast-action) yeast, skip step 1. Just add to the flour in step 2, along with the warm water.

Check that you are not using yeast beyond its best-before date.

1 In a small bowl, whisk the warm water and dried active yeast until the yeast has dissolved. Let it stand for 5 minutes. After this time the yeast should be foamy, which indicates that it is still active. (If you are using instant yeast, skip this step.)

2 Mix the flours, salt, sugar and olive oil in a large mixing bowl, then add the yeast and water. Using your hands, or a mixer fitted with a dough hook, knead until you have a sticky, shaggy dough. If it feels too wet, sprinkle in a bit more flour.

3 Spread a thin layer of olive oil (about 1 teaspoon) around the sides of the dough. Cover the bowl with a clean tea towel and leave to rise.

4 Slow ferment in a large sealed container – 24 hours in the fridge. Quick ferment – 1½ hours in a warm place. Medium ferment – 8 hours at room temperature.

5 Meanwhile, to make the kale pesto, put the kale in a bowl and cover with boiling water for 1–2 minutes, until soft and bright green. Drain, then cover the kale with cold water and leave for 2–3 minutes. Drain thoroughly, then place in a food processor or blender with the toasted nuts or seeds, olive oil, nutritional yeast, lemon juice and zest, salt and pepper. Blend until slightly chunky; set aside.

6 Preheat the oven to its hottest setting (at least 240°C/220°C fan/gas 9) for 20 minutes.

Fun facts Pizza is the first meal I can remember having (I think I was 4 years old). In my first job, I was the doughboy in a pizza restaurant. My DNA is 50 per cent pizza.

 4–8
 30 mins
 15 mins
 Up to 5 days
 Up to 1 month

7 Dust your hands with flour and tip the dough onto a floured surface. Starting at the centre of the dough, using your fingertips, press out the dough to 2cm thick, turning and gently stretching as you press. Put the dough onto a rimmed baking sheet, about 40 x 30cm, and shape it to fit. Let it rest for 5–10 minutes to rise gently.

8 With lightly oiled fingers, dimple the dough and then spread a thin layer (about 4 tablespoons) of the tomato sauce to the edges. Bake for 3 minutes.

9 Remove from the oven and add a slightly thicker layer of tomato sauce (about 150g) and the parmesan. Lightly drizzle with extra-virgin olive oil, then bake for 8–10 minutes, or until the crust is golden brown and crispy.

10 Meanwhile, in a mixing bowl, toss the rocket and herbs with the balsamic vinegar and chilli flakes.

11 Remove the pizza from the oven and leave to cool for 5 minutes. Lightly run a spatula around the edges of the crust, then transfer to a cutting board and cut into squares. Add more grated parmesan and spoonfuls of kale pesto and top with the rocket and herbs.

Crispy Kale Udon Noodles and Peanut Butter Miso Dressing

Everyone needs a quick, hearty noodle dish in their lives, and this is it! Using mostly ingredients already in your cupboards it's a perfect balance of fresh, crunch, heat and creaminess – and it is 100 per cent satisfying. Kale provides a crispy layer, but if you don't have kale, use steamed spinach or peas instead and skip the baking step.

100g kale, leaves stripped from stems and roughly torn
2 tbsp extra-virgin olive oil
2 tbsp nutritional yeast
½ tsp salt
200g udon noodles
1 tbsp smooth peanut butter
1 tbsp fresh ginger, grated
1 garlic clove, grated
1 tsp sesame oil
1 tbsp white miso
zest and juice of 1 lime
½ tsp chilli flakes
1 tsp maple syrup or light brown sugar
35g toasted peanuts or almonds, crushed
1 baby cucumber, cut into thin matchsticks
½ tsp sesame seeds, toasted
pinch of salt

Tips Use the kale stems for Fridge Greens Fusilli (page 160) or Stems and Herbs Pesto (page 156).

More bulk? Add crispy tofu from page 105.

Make ahead: prepare the sauce the day before or double the quantity to use again later in the week.

Look for gluten-free noodles if you prefer.

1   Preheat the oven to 150ºC/130ºC fan/gas 2. Line 2 baking sheets with baking parchment.

2   In a large bowl, toss and lightly massage the kale with the olive oil, nutritional yeast and salt until evenly coated.

3   Spread the kale over the baking sheets and cook for about 8 minutes, flipping halfway through, until the kale is crispy and dark around the edges.

4   Meanwhile, bring a large pan of salted water to the boil and cook the noodles according to the packet instructions. Drain thoroughly. Transfer the noodles to a large bowl.

5   In a separate bowl or jug, whisk together the peanut butter, ginger, garlic, sesame oil, miso, lime juice and half the zest, the chilli flakes and maple syrup, until smooth. If the dressing is too thick, add 1 teaspoon of water to loosen. Pour most of the dressing over the noodles and mix gently to coat.

6   Fold in half of the crispy kale, then serve topped with the remaining crispy kale, the crushed nuts, cucumber, remaining lime zest, the rest of peanut butter miso dressing and the sesame seeds and salt.

 2   15 mins   10 mins   1–3 days   Up to 1 month

Super Green Pancakes

A green smoothie magically turns into a stack of pancakes – that's my kind of breakfast! Colourful, healthy and fun. If you're not wild about the taste of spinach, don't fret – you won't taste it. A fan favourite and soon to be yours. Have fun with the toppings!

60g spinach
2 ripe bananas
320ml milk
225g plain flour
1½ tsp baking powder
½ tsp ground cinnamon
½ tsp salt
1 tsp vanilla extract
2–3 tsp vegetable oil (optional)

To serve
your choice of toppings: fresh fruits,
  yoghurt, nut butter, toasted coconut
  flakes, toasted pumpkin seeds,
  maple syrup

1 In a food processor or blender, blitz the spinach, bananas and milk until smooth.

2 In a large mixing bowl, add the flour, baking powder, cinnamon and salt and stir to combine. Add the spinach and banana mixture, along with the vanilla, and stir until the batter is thick but pourable. If too thick, add a small splash of milk to loosen the batter. If too loose, stir in 1 tablespoon of flour at a time to thicken slightly.

3 Heat a non-stick frying pan over medium heat (depending on your pan, you may like to add a little oil to prevent the pancakes from sticking). Once the pan is hot, add half-ladlefuls of the batter to make small pancakes. Cook for 1–1½ minutes, until the pancakes rise and bubbles appear on the surface. Flip and cook on the other side for 1–2 minutes. Keep warm while you cook the remaining batter.

4 To serve, stack the pancakes and add your favourite toppings. I went for fresh blueberries, coconut yoghurt, almond butter, toasted coconut flakes, pumpkin seeds and a drizzle of maple syrup.

Tips Do not flatten the pancakes with the spatula as they cook: allow them to rise to nice, fluffy pancakes.

Save leftover batter to make savoury crepes for dinner.

Use gluten-free flour and baking powder if you need a gluten-free option.

 12 pancakes | 5 mins | 10–15 mins | Up to 3 days | ❄ Up to 1 month

6– Fungi & Alliums

Mushrooms
Onion
Garlic

Mushroom Ravioli with Tofu Asparagus Purée

Don't be put off making this because you think home-made pasta is too difficult. Just follow the steps and you'll be surprised how easy it is – it's failproof! The ravioli has a rich mushroom filling and it's served on an elegant asparagus cream, finished with a parsley-lemon oil. Make it for friends and family when you want to really impress. *Photo overleaf*

Pasta
400g 00 flour, plus more for dusting (or semolina for dusting)
pinch of ground turmeric
200g aquafaba
oat milk (optional)
salt

Filling
2 tbsp olive oil
400g mixed mushrooms, roughly chopped
2 garlic cloves, grated
1 tbsp thyme leaves
200g cream cheese
zest of 1 lemon

Asparagus cream
350g asparagus
340g silken tofu
20g fresh parsley
zest and juice of 1 lemon
2 tbsp nutritional yeast
2 tbsp tahini
2 tsp Dijon mustard
4 tbsp olive oil
2 garlic cloves, finely sliced
4 tbsp toasted pine nuts, to serve

1   First make the pasta. Add the flour to a bowl or a stand mixer, along with the turmeric and a pinch of salt, and mix well. Make a well in the middle of the flour and pour in the aquafaba. Use a fork to draw it together. Don't worry if it looks a little dry, it'll come together. Use your hands to knead the mixture, then tip it onto a lightly floured work surface and knead for a further minute until you have a soft ball of dough. Place in a bowl, cover with a damp clean tea towel and set aside.

2   Make the mushroom filling. Heat the oil in a frying pan over high heat. Add the mushrooms and a generous pinch of salt, and fry for 5–10 minutes, until the mushrooms are golden, and all their liquid has evaporated from the pan. Add the garlic and thyme leaves, cook for 1 minute, then remove from the heat and tip into a bowl with the cream cheese and lemon zest, stirring to combine. Set aside to cool or pop it in the fridge until you're ready to fill your pasta.

3   Make the asparagus cream. Bring a pan of salted water to the boil. Remove any very woody ends from the asparagus (save them for stock or blend them to make a soup). Cut the asparagus stems in half, separating the stems from the tips; set the tips aside for later. Cook the stems in the boiling water for 3–5 minutes, until a knife slides through them easily. Drain and add to a high-speed blender with the tofu, parsley stems (save the leaves for later), the lemon juice, nutritional yeast, tahini and Dijon mustard. Blitz until smooth, set aside and keep warm.

 4   40 mins   15–25 mins   Up to 5 days   Up to 1 month

Fungi & Alliums

4 Line a tray with a little flour or semolina and lightly flour the work surface. Cut the pasta dough into quarters. Take one quarter and roll through your pasta-making machine – you want to take it to 2–3mm thickness, so it's thick enough to hold the filling. Roll to a sheet approx. 40cm long, then cut the sheet into 3 rectangles on the work surface.

5 For each rectangle, add 2–3 heaped tablespoons of the filling on one side, leaving a generous border, then fold the other side over and press to seal with your fingers. Use a knife to neaten the edges – and use a little oat milk to help them stick if you think it needs it. Set aside on the lined tray and repeat with the other rectangles, making 3 large ravioli per person. Repeat with the rest of the dough.

6 Bring a large pan of salted water to the boil. While it's coming to the boil, add the 4 tablespoons of olive oil to a large frying pan over a high heat. Add the reserved asparagus tips and fry for 2 minutes, then add the garlic, fry for 1 minute, then remove from the heat. Finely chop the parsley leaves and add to the pan along with the lemon zest. Season well.

7 Drop the pasta into the boiling water and cook for 3–4 minutes, until soft, then use a slotted spoon to slosh them into the asparagus pan.

8 Spread the asparagus cream onto the base on your serving bowls. Top with the pasta and spoon over the asparagus tips and parsley-lemon oil from the pan. Scatter with the toasted pine nuts and serve.

Tips When you seal the pasta, make sure to press around the filling to release any air otherwise it could burst open as it cooks.

You can, of course, use bought pasta and serve it with the mushroom and asparagus cream sauce.

Fun fact The first time I made pasta I was 5 years old, then I didn't make it for 20 years.

Crispy Mushroom Risotto

This risotto is rich, creamy and packed with flavour, with a topping of crispy mushrooms. Don't worry if you can't find shiitake mushrooms: I've made this risotto with chestnut mushrooms and it was still delicious.

1 tbsp + 1 tsp olive oil
3 tbsp butter
1 onion, finely chopped
2 celery sticks, finely chopped
3 garlic cloves, thinly sliced
250g shiitake mushrooms, cut into
   5mm slices
1 tsp brown sugar
2 tsp soy sauce or tamari
2 tsp freshly chopped thyme
200g arborio rice
200ml white wine
800ml veg stock, warmed
60g parmesan, grated
zest and juice of 1 lemon
2 tbsp freshly chopped parsley
salt and black pepper

1   Preheat the oven to 200°C/180°C fan/gas 6. Line a baking sheet with baking parchment.

2   In a large pan, heat 1 tablespoon of olive oil and 2 tablespoons of butter over low heat, add the onion, celery and garlic, season with salt and black pepper, and cook for about 10 minutes, stirring occasionally, until soft.

3   Meanwhile, put the mushrooms in a large mixing bowl, add 1 teaspoon of olive oil, the brown sugar, soy sauce and 1 teaspoon of chopped thyme and toss to combine. Spread the mushrooms evenly over the lined baking sheet and bake for 15–20 minutes, flipping halfway through, until crispy and slightly charred. Remove from the oven and set aside.

4   Increase the heat under the onion mixture to medium, add the rice and stir to coat, then add the wine and cook for 2–3 minutes, stirring occasionally.

5   Once the wine has almost evaporated, add a ladleful of veg stock to the rice mixture and stir until absorbed. Continue to add the stock, a ladleful at a time, stirring continuously, for about 30 minutes, until the rice is cooked. You may need to adjust the heat to keep the mixture at a steady simmer.

6   Remove the risotto from the heat and stir in half of the parmesan, the lemon juice, half of the crispy mushrooms, 1 tablespoon of butter, 1 tablespoon of the chopped parsley and the remaining thyme.

7   Serve in bowls, topped with the remaining crispy mushrooms, parsley, parmesan, lemon zest and a pinch of salt and black pepper.

Tip Use tamari (rather than soy sauce) for a gluten-free dish.

 4   15 mins   45 mins   1 day   Up to 1 month

Pulled Mushroom Tacos, Avocado and Tomato Salsa

The hero of this dish is of course the king oyster mushrooms, which when shredded almost exactly resemble the texture of succulent pulled pork. I once worked in a Spanish-Asian restaurant in New York, which served incredible pulled pork tacos and I wanted to replicate the meatiness and flavour of that special dish. Top the tacos with generous amount of cooling creamy avocado salsa.

260g king oyster mushrooms
4 tbsp vegetable oil
2 garlic cloves, finely chopped
1 tbsp ancho chilli paste
½ tsp ground cumin
½ tsp chilli powder
generous pinch of salt
  and black pepper
8–12 corn or flour tortillas,
  warmed, to serve

Avocado salsa
1 large tomato, diced
2 spring onions, thinly sliced
1 jalapeño pepper, seeded
  and finely chopped
1 large avocado, diced
4 tbsp freshly chopped coriander,
  including stems
zest and juice of 1 lime
pinch of salt

1 First, make the avocado salsa by gently folding all the ingredients together in a small bowl. Leave to one side while you prepare the pulled mushrooms.

2 Shred the oyster mushrooms into pieces. Heat the oil in a large non-stick frying pan over medium–high heat and cook half of the mushrooms in a single layer for 10–12 minutes, stirring occasionally, until the edges starting to char. For the last 3–5 minutes, add half the garlic and ancho chilli paste, stirring to combine. Using tongs, transfer the mushrooms to a bowl. Repeat with the rest of the mushrooms.

3 Once the second batch of mushrooms is cooked, toss all the mushrooms with the cumin, chilli powder, salt and black pepper.

4 Serve the mushrooms with warm tortillas and the avocado salsa.

Tips Use gluten-free corn tortillas if you prefer.

You can add any other leftover mushrooms to the mix.

 2–4   10 mins   20–25 mins   Up to 3 days

Easy Bean and Mushroom Casserole

Make this bean and mushroom casserole as a side dish, or make ahead to enjoy as a main for those evenings when you don't have time to cook. Comforting and delicious, topped with golden cheese and crispy breadcrumbs, this is one of my favourite dishes to make.

400g chestnut mushrooms, cut into 1cm slices
4 garlic cloves, finely chopped
2 tbsp extra-virgin olive oil
1 tsp dried oregano
1 x 400g tin cannellini beans, rinsed and drained
1 x 400g tin chopped tomatoes
2 tsp roughly chopped fresh thyme
60g mozzarella, shredded
60g breadcrumbs (home-made from a stale loaf)
salt and black pepper
garlic bread (try my Cheesy Garlic Bread, page 199), to serve

1   Preheat the oven to 190°C/170°C fan/gas 5

2   In an ovenproof frying pan, combine the mushrooms with half of the garlic, the olive oil, oregano and a generous pinch of salt and black pepper. Cook over medium heat for about 10 minutes, stirring often, until the mushrooms are lightly golden brown and they begin to reduce in size.

3   Remove the pan from the heat. Stir in the beans, tomatoes, thyme and the remaining garlic. Scatter over the mozzarella. Sprinkle the breadcrumbs over the top and bake for 20–25 minutes, until the mixture is bubbling and the cheese is lightly golden brown.

4   Leave to cool for a few minutes before serving with my cheesy garlic bread on page 199.

Tip Use gluten-free breadcrumbs if you need a gluten-free option, or use my Crispy Garlic Breadcrumbs from page 30 or the garlicky breadcrumbs on page 90.

 4–6   10 mins   35 mins   Up to 3 days   Up to 1 month

Mushroom Masala and Crispy Cardamon Rice

I don't want to say that this dish was created because of my love of alliteration ... but it may have played a part! Chunky mushrooms and juicy tomatoes are all wrapped up in the familiar aromatics of a rich masala sauce. Served with baked coconut rice, spiked with cloves, cardamom and cinnamon, this has quickly become a weeknight go-to.

2 tbsp neutral oil (e.g. groundnut, sunflower or vegetable)
1 onion, finely diced
3 garlic cloves, minced
1 tbsp grated fresh ginger
1 tsp ground turmeric
1 tsp ground cumin
1 tbsp garam masala
1 tsp chilli powder
1 x 400g tin chopped tomatoes
400g mixed mushrooms
 (I use an exotic mix; any larger ones sliced)
120ml full-fat coconut cream
1 lime

Baked rice
300g basmati or jasmine rice
400ml coconut milk
200ml veg stock
4–6 cardamon pods
1 stick cinnamon or
 1 tsp ground cinnamon
salt and black pepper

To serve
4 tbsp fresh mint
4 tbsp fresh coriander
coconut cream or yoghurt
My Fragrant Flatbreads on page 206

1 Preheat the oven to 180°C/160°C fan/gas 4.

2 Rinse the rice under cold running water until the water runs clear. Drain, then tip into a baking dish with the coconut milk, stock, cardamon and cinnamon. Season with salt and black pepper, cover with foil and bake for 40–45 minutes, until the rice is cooked through, and all the liquid has been absorbed. Remove from the oven and set aside.

3 Meanwhile, heat 1 tablespoon of the oil in a large saucepan over medium heat. Fry the onion with a generous pinch of salt for 5 minutes, until soft. Add the garlic, ginger and the spices, and cook for 2 minutes, stirring occasionally. Add the chopped tomatoes, reduce to a simmer, cover with a lid and cook for 20 minutes.

4 In a frying pan over high heat, dry fry the mushrooms, stirring often, for 5–7 minutes, until the mushrooms have released their liquid. Reduce the heat to medium, add the remaining oil, and cook, stirring, for 3–5 minutes until slightly crispy around the edges.

5 Stir the coconut cream into the curry, followed by the crispy mushrooms. Taste and season well, adding the juice of half the lime. Cut the remaining lime half into wedges to serve.

6 Serve the curry with the rice, scattered with the fresh herbs and drizzled with coconut cream. Serve with flatbreads and lime wedges on the side.

 4   10 mins   40–45 mins   Up to 5 days   Up to 1 month **GF**

Fungi & Alliums

Mushroom Pad Thai

I love pad Thai! I think it's because of the unbeatable combination of crunchy beansprouts and peanuts, silky noodles and fresh herbs with the salty sweet-and-tangy sauce and fiery ginger. In my version, I've used two types of mushrooms for extra texture and flavour. Pulled together quickly, it's like magic happening in the kitchen.

200g flat rice noodles
1 tbsp vegetable oil
300g mushrooms, quartered
3 spring onions, finely sliced
2 garlic cloves, finely sliced
1 tbsp fresh ginger, cut
   into matchsticks
150g beansprouts
salt and black pepper

Sauce
zest and juice of 1–2 limes
2 tbsp tamarind paste
4 tbsp soy sauce or tamari
2 tbsp brown sugar
1 tbsp white miso

To serve
a handful of salted peanuts, crushed
4 tbsp fresh coriander leaves
4 tbsp fresh mint leaves

1 Cover the rice noodles with boiling water and set aside for 10–15 minutes, until softened. Drain the noodles, rinse and leave to sit in a bowl of cold water (this stops them clumping together).

2 Make the sauce. Whisk all the ingredients together; add the zest and juice of 1 lime to begin with, then taste and add the zest and juice of the other if needed.

3 Heat the oil in a large frying pan or wok over high heat. Add the mushrooms with a generous pinch of salt and fry for 5–10 minutes, until golden.

4 Add most of the spring onions, the garlic and ginger and toss well. Use tongs to add the rice noodles, along with the beansprouts. Keep tossing, then add the sauce and coat well. Taste and season with salt and black pepper.

5 Serve topped with the crushed peanuts, fresh herb leaves and remaining spring onions. Serve with any leftover lime, cut into wedges, on the side.

Tip Use tamari (rather than soy sauce) for a gluten-free dish.

 4
 20 mins
 15 mins
 Up to 5 days
 Up to 1 month
GF

Takeaway-style Mushrooms and 'Egg' Noodles

Mushrooms are the hero of this satisfying, sweet and salty dish, so if you're craving 'egg' noodles, it's so much better than ordering in. The secret is the bicarbonate of soda which magically combines with the starchy water to produce that distinctive egg-like flavour. To make the meal more substantial, top with crispy tofu or add more veg.

150g shiitake mushrooms
1 tsp olive oil
2 tsp soy sauce or tamari
2 garlic cloves, finely chopped
1 tsp maple syrup
200g spaghetti
2 tsp bicarbonate of soda

Sauce
3 tbsp soy sauce or tamari
2 tbsp toasted sesame oil
1 tbsp smooth peanut butter
2 tsp rice vinegar
2 tsp sugar
1 tbsp grated fresh ginger
1 tsp chilli flakes

To serve
40g roasted peanuts, chopped
1 baby cucumber, cut into matchsticks

1   Preheat the oven to 200°C/180°C fan/gas 6. Line a baking sheet with baking parchment.

2   Put the mushrooms in a mixing bowl, add the olive oil, soy sauce, garlic and maple syrup and toss to combine. Spread evenly over the baking sheet and bake for about 12 minutes, until crispy. Remove from the heat and set aside.

3   Meanwhile, bring a pan of water to the boil and cook the spaghetti for about 10 minutes or until tender and cooked all the way through. About halfway through cooking, add 1 teaspoon of bicarbonate of soda at a time – the bicarbonate of soda will make the water bubble. Turn off the heat and let the spaghetti sit in the water for about 5–7 minutes, until doubled in thickness. Drain and place in a mixing bowl.

4   Put all the sauce ingredients into a small jar or bowl; close the lid and shake vigorously, or whisk until smooth. Pour half of the sauce over the noodles and toss.

5   Serve the noodles in bowls, topped with the crispy mushrooms, chopped peanuts, cucumber and a drizzle of the sauce.

Tips Use gluten-free pasta and tamari (rather than soy sauce) for a gluten-free dish.

You can use any type of pasta or noodle for this.

Be mindful when you add the bicarb: it will bubble up like a science project – you may need to reduce the heat to prevent spillage.

 2   10 mins   20 mins   Up to 3 days   Up to 1 month

Fungi & Alliums

Meaty Mushroom Mince Burgers

These burgers are for the bros in your life! Already chunky and meaty from the mince, I've made them next-level juicy and satisfying with extra mushrooms. Perfect for barbecues, picnics and relaxed summertime vibes, pile these high with toppings and make them your own. Beer keg optional.

1 tbsp flaxseed
200g chestnut or portobello
    mushrooms, roughly chopped
2 tbsp olive oil
1 onion, finely diced
2 garlic cloves, grated
300g mince
2 tbsp nutritional yeast
30g breadcrumbs
4 slices smoked gouda
salt and black pepper

To serve
4 tbsp mayo
4 burger buns
2 little gem lettuce, leaves
    pulled apart
4 tomatoes, sliced
pickles or gherkins
1 red onion, sliced
ketchup
mustard

1 In a small bowl, combine the flaxseed or chia seeds with 1 tablespoon of water. Set aside to thicken to a jelly-like consistency.

2 In a large frying pan over high heat, dry fry the mushrooms for 5–7 minutes, until the mushrooms have released most of their liquid. This gives them a slightly meatier texture. Tip into a bowl.

3 In the same frying pan, reduce the heat to medium, add 1 tablespoon of oil and fry the onion with a generous pinch each of salt and pepper for 5 minutes, until soft. Add the garlic, cook for a further minute, then tip into the bowl with the mushrooms. Add the mince, flaxseed mixture, nutritional yeast and breadcrumbs.

4 Use your hands to bring the mixture together then roll into 4 large burger patties. Flatten them a little in the palms of your hands, then place on a baking sheet lined with baking parchment and chill in the fridge for 30 minutes to firm up.

5 When ready to serve, heat the remaining oil in a large frying pan over a medium–high heat. Fry the burgers for 3–4 minutes on one side, then flip over and immediately top with a slice of the cheese. Cook for 3–4 minutes, until the cheese is melting. Encourage the cheese to melt by adding a splash of water to the pan and covering with a lid!

6 Spread the mayo on the base of the burger buns, top with the burger patties, followed by lettuce, tomato, pickles and red onion. Spread some ketchup and mustard on the top bun and close the lid.

Tip You could make 8 smaller patties instead and serve up mini meaty sliders!

 4
 15 mins
 20 mins
 Up to 5 days
 Up to 1 month

Fungi & Alliums

Extra Crunchy Onion Rings

A fan favourite, with over 2 million views, these are the best crispy onion rings you'll ever make. Don't be tempted to take them out of the oven too soon: bake until they're golden brown and crispy. These onion rings never get the chance to sit around for long. *Photo overleaf*

2–3 large onions
flaky sea salt for sprinkling

Batter
65g plain flour or gluten-free flour
150ml milk of your choice
1 tbsp apple cider vinegar
1 tsp baking powder
½ tsp chilli powder
¼ tsp ground turmeric
black pepper

Breadcrumb mix
100g panko breadcrumbs
2 tbsp cornmeal
½ tsp chilli powder
¼ tsp thyme (fresh or dried)
¼ tsp ground turmeric

1 Preheat the oven to 220°C/200°C fan/gas 7. Line a baking sheet with baking parchment.

2 Slice the ends off each onion and carefully slice the onions into 1cm-thick rounds.

3 To make the batter, in a mixing bowl, whisk all the ingredients together with a pinch of black pepper until smooth and pourable.

4 For the breadcrumb mix, mix all the dry ingredients together with a pinch of black pepper then divide between 2 separate bowls: keep one bowl to the side – this will come in handy when the first bowl of breadcrumbs gets a bit soggy from the batter.

5 Dip each onion ring in the batter and allow any excess batter to drip off. Then place the onion ring in the breadcrumb mix and coat well. Place the coated onion rings on the lined baking sheet and bake for 8–10 minutes, or until golden brown and crispy.

6 Serve immediately with a sprinkle of flaky sea salt and a dipping sauce of your choice. I eat mine with ketchup or mayo.

Tips Perfect with my Spicy Grilled Bean Burger (page 00), Ultimate Veggie Burger (page 00) or alongside a salad.

Can be made in an air-fryer.

Save the onion skins and trimmed ends in a bag or container in the fridge or freezer to make a veg stock (page 260).

Don't store any leftovers in the fridge – they will go soft.

 4   10 mins   10 mins

Caramelised Onion and Miso Mushroom Rigatoni

I'm a big fan of pasta and in this dish, I wanted to bring it together with all the flavours of a classic French onion soup! Sweet, caramelised onions, thyme and a little mustard and chilli for heat, with added mushrooms for a chunkier, meatier texture. It's topped with crispy, fried breadcrumbs and parmesan – just like the melted cheese toasts you get on the traditional soup.

2 tbsp olive oil
3 tbsp butter
3 onions, thinly sliced
1 shallot, thinly sliced
2 tbsp freshly chopped thyme,
    plus more to serve
½ tsp salt
¼ tsp black pepper
1 tsp sugar (optional)
pinch of chilli flakes
2 tsp white wine vinegar
225g white or chestnut
    mushrooms, sliced
2 garlic cloves, finely chopped
380g dried rigatoni or pasta
    of your choice
50g dried breadcrumbs
    (home-made or panko)
1 tsp Dijon mustard
1 tbsp white miso (optional)
2 tbsp roughly chopped fresh parsley
2 tbsp grated parmesan

Tips Use gluten-free pasta and breadcrumbs if you prefer.

If you have some of my Garlic and Lemon Pagrattato (page 200) to hand, use that instead of frying the breadcrumbs in step 5.

1 Heat 1 tablespoon of the olive oil and the butter in a large non-stick frying pan over medium heat until the butter has melted. Stir in the onions and shallot, then leave to cook undisturbed for 3 minutes. If the onions and shallot start to brown, lower the heat.

2 Stir in the thyme, salt, pepper, sugar, if using, and chilli flakes. Continue cooking over a low heat for 15–20 minutes, stirring every 3 minutes, until the onions have collapsed and resemble onion jam.

3 Add the vinegar and mushrooms and cook for 3–5 minutes, until the mushrooms are soft. Stir in the garlic for the last minute of cooking.

4 Meanwhile, bring a large pan of salted water to the boil and cook the pasta according to the packet instructions. Drain, reserving 2 tablespoons of the pasta cooking water.

5 Heat the remaining olive oil in a small pan over medium heat. Cook the breadcrumbs for about 3 minutes, stirring often, until golden brown and crispy.

6 Add the mustard, miso, if using, and reserved pasta water to the onion and mushroom mixture, stir well to combine, then fold through the pasta.

7 Serve in bowls, with a sprinkling of crispy breadcrumbs, fresh thyme, parsley and grated parmesan.

 4   15 mins   30–35 mins   Up to 3 days   Up to 1 month

Quick Garlic Chilli Ramen

I asked my audience how much time they usually have to cook, and most people came back saying 15 minutes! So here we are: a recipe that I think is actually on the table closer to 10 minutes. Sautéing the spring onions brings out their sweetness while the fresh ginger keeps things fiery. This is such a simple dish for when you're short on time but don't want to compromise on taste. Add crispy tofu, such as my Killer Tofu Ground 'Beef' on page 128, or steamed spinach, broccoli or peas if you want to bulk it up.

25g fresh ginger, cut into
   thin matchsticks
4 garlic cloves, finely grated
6 spring onions, very thinly sliced
100ml vegetable oil
2 tbsp soy sauce, tamari
   or teriyaki sauce
1 tbsp rice vinegar
1 tsp toasted sesame oil
½ tsp sugar
½ tsp black pepper
200g ramen noodles
1–2 tsp toasted white or black
   sesame seeds
Quick Garlic Chilli Oil (page 00),
   or crushed chillies in vinegar
   (shop-bought)
lime wedges, to serve

1 Put the ginger, garlic and half of the spring onions in a large bowl.

2 Heat the oil in a frying pan over medium–high heat for 2 minutes. Pour the hot oil over the spring onion mixture and set aside for 1–2 minutes, until the spring onion is vibrantly green and soft. Stir in the soy sauce, vinegar, sesame oil, sugar and black pepper. Set aside for 10 minutes.

3 Meanwhile, cook the noodles according to the packet instructions. Drain well, then toss the noodles in a few spoonfuls of the spring onion sauce.

4 Serve with lime wedges and topped with toasted sesame seeds, the remaining spring onions and some quick garlic chilli oil or crushed chillies in vinegar.

 2–4   10 mins   10 mins   Up to 3 days   Up to 1 month

Tenderstem and Cream Cheese on Toast with Pickled Broccoli

Slightly softened, charred broccoli sits on cool, cream cheese base, then topped with the sweet-acidic crunch of the broccoli stem pickle. Two different types of broccoli for the price of one! Serve one toast each as a starter or cut into smaller pieces as a party appetiser.

400g Tenderstem broccoli
juice of 2 lemons
2 tbsp capers
1 shallot, finely diced
1 tsp sugar
2 tbsp olive oil, plus more to serve
4 thick slices of sourdough
120g cream cheese
3 tbsp pine nuts, toasted
  and roughly chopped
handful of fresh dill or parsley,
  finely chopped
pinch of red chilli flakes
salt and black pepper

1   Finely slice the stems of the Tenderstem, leaving 10cm at the top. Put the stems in a bowl with the lemon juice, capers, shallot, sugar and a pinch of salt. Toss everything together and set aside.

2   Preheat the grill to high. Tip the broccoli heads onto a baking sheet. Drizzle with 1 tablespoon of the olive oil and season with salt and black pepper. Slide under the grill for about 8 minutes, depending on the thickness of your broccoli, until slightly charred.

3   Meanwhile, toast the slices of bread. Spread each slice of toast with 2 tablespoons of the cream cheese, top with the charred broccoli and spoon the pickled stems over the top. Finish with the toasted pine nuts, herbs, a pinch of chilli flakes and a drizzle of olive oil.

 4   10 mins   10 mins   Up to 3 days

Cheesy Garlic Bread

With the perfect butter, cheese, garlic ratio, and deliciously soft bread in the middle, make this recipe once and I guarantee you'll keep coming back to it! Dunk this cheesy garlic bread in soups or stews, or serve alongside pasta or salad.

6 garlic cloves, grated
100g butter, at room temperature
1 tsp Dijon mustard
75g parmesan, grated
zest and juice of ½ lemon
2 tsp dried or freshly chopped oregano
2 tsp freshly chopped parsley
½ tsp chilli flakes
½ tsp salt
½ tsp black pepper
1 large baguette or any loaf-style
   of bread

1 In a small mixing bowl, mash the garlic, butter, mustard, parmesan, lemon juice and zest, oregano, parsley and chilli flakes. Season with the salt and pepper.

2 Preheat the grill to medium. Line a baking sheet with baking parchment.

3 Slice the baguette in half lengthways, then into quarters. Place, cut-side down, on the lined baking sheet and grill for 2 minutes. Leave to cool on the baking tray for 2 minutes, then spread the cut sides with the garlic butter. Grill for about 3 minutes, until beginning to bubble. Leave to cool slightly before slicing into 5cm pieces and serving.

Tips Save any leftover garlic butter and toss with pasta, serve on steamed veg or use to sauté mushrooms to go on toast.

To reheat leftover garlic bread (you won't see this in my home!), place on a baking sheet in a preheated oven at and bake for 5-7 minutes until warm and crunchy.

 8   10 mins   5 mins   Up to 5 days   Up to 1 month

Garlic and Lemon Pangrattato

Italians often top their dishes with dried breadcrumbs to add a layer of crunch, and it's a great use for any type of stale leftover bread. I use my garlicky version – made with cornflakes for even more crunchy flavour! – scattered over pasta or noodle dishes, in salads and on gratins. To give it an Asian-style spin add a little freshly grated ginger with the garlic and substitute lemon for lime.

3 tbsp butter
4–5 garlic cloves, grated
½ tsp dried thyme
150g dried breadcrumbs
 (home-made or panko)
30g unsweetened cornflakes,
 crushed (optional)
zest of 1 lemon
1 tbsp fresh parsley, finely chopped
salt and black pepper

1 Melt the butter in a non-stick frying pan over medium–low heat. Stir in the garlic and cook for 2 minutes.

2 Add the dried thyme, breadcrumbs and cornflakes, if using, and stir to coat in the garlicky butter. Keeping a careful eye on it so it doesn't burn and, stirring often, cook the breadcrumb mixture for 4–5 minutes, until golden brown. Remove from heat and toss with lemon zest and fresh parsley.

3 Season with salt and black pepper and tip onto a baking tray to cool. Store in an airtight container for up to 7 days.

4 Serve the pangrattato over any pasta dish or over simply cooked veg dishes.

Tips Use gluten-free breadcrumbs and cornflakes if you prefer.

Save the crumbs from the bottom of your cornflake box to add to this recipe.

 4–6   5 mins   10 mins   Up to 7 days*
*air-tight container

Rich Garlic and Onion Broth

Onions and garlic are often 'forgotten' and when you find them, they have often softened or have green shoots budding through the skins. You can remove the green shoots and carry on, but I take this as an opportunity to make a supremely savoury stock. The flavour is intense and delicious. Great to keep on hand and stored in the fridge or freezer. Use in recipes that ask for stock, such as my Crispy Mushroom Risotto (page 178) or Creamy Leek and Parsnip Soup (page 22), or add noodles for a warming and grounding meal.

1 bulb of garlic, not peeled,
  lightly crushed
1 onion (any kind), not
  peeled, quartered
2 tbsp extra-virgin olive oil
1 tbsp white miso (optional)
1.5 litres water
a handful of herbs (e.g. parsley,
  basil and/or sage)
salt and black pepper
cooked noodles, to serve (optional)

1   If you can see green shoots at the tops of the garlic or onion, remove and discard them.

2   Heat the oil in a large saucepan over medium–low heat. Add the whole bulb of garlic and cook for 5–7 minutes, turning it over in the oil until evenly golden brown all over. Add the onion and miso, if using, and cook for another 5 minutes, stirring occasionally, until the onion is soft.

3   Pour in the water and give everything a good stir to combine. Turn the heat up to bring to the broth to the boil, then reduce to a simmer. Stir through the herbs, and leave to simmer for 20–30 minutes, until the broth is fragrant and a deep golden brown. Season with salt and black pepper.

4   Strain the broth and serve hot, with added cooked noodles if you like. Alternatively, leave to cool completely before storing in a sealed container in the fridge for 2 weeks, or freeze in ice cube trays for up to 3 months.

Tips For a deeper, richer umami flavour, add 50-60g mushrooms.

Compost the cooked veg or leave in the food waste collection bin if you have one.

 about 1.5 litres

 5 mins

 35–45 mins

 Up to 2 weeks

 Up to 3 months

Roasted Onion and Leek Dip

This roasted onion dip is a real crowd-pleaser. It's easy to put together and goes well with crisps or with crunchy raw veg such as carrots, cauliflower florets and celery. It is also perfect for spreading in sandwiches and burgers.

2 onions, thinly sliced
1 large leek, thinly sliced, including the green top
4 spring onions, roots removed
3 garlic cloves, chopped
1 tbsp olive oil
pinch of salt
¼ tsp black pepper
zest and juice of ½ lemon
120g mayo
120g yoghurt
1 tbsp milk (optional)
2 fresh thyme sprigs, chopped
1 tbsp snipped fresh chives

1 Preheat the oven to 180°C/160°C fan/gas 4. Line a baking tin with baking parchment.

2 Put the onions, leek, spring onions and garlic in the baking tin and toss with the olive oil, salt and pepper. Roast for about 15 minutes, until soft and lightly charred. Remove from the oven and leave to cool.

3 Tip the roasted veg into a food processor and add the lemon juice and zest, mayo and yoghurt. Pulse until the mixture is smooth but slightly chunky. If too thick, add 1 tablespoon of milk to loosen the mixture.

4 Serve in a bowl, sprinkled with thyme and chives.

 8
 10 mins
 15 mins
 Up to 5 days
 Up to 1 month
GF

7– Non-dairy

Milk
Yoghurt

Fragrant Flatbreads

I love eating with my hands – it's a really fun and playful way to appreciate food in a whole new way. These light, fluffy breads are the perfect vehicle for scooping up leftover sauce or curry – try them with my Easy Spinach and Chickpea Curry on page 159 or the Tofu Butter 'Chicken' on page 124.

60ml warm water
1 tbsp maple syrup
1 tsp dried active yeast
180ml warm milk (I use oat)
200g yoghurt (I use coconut yoghurt)
500g plain flour, plus more for dusting
1½ tsp baking powder
1 tsp bicarbonate of soda
¼ tsp salt
8 tbsp butter, melted
2 garlic cloves, grated
40g mixed fresh herbs (e.g. basil, parsley, chives, dill), chopped

1   In a large mixing bowl, whisk together the warm water, maple syrup and yeast. Set aside for 5 minutes, until foamy.

2   Add the milk, yoghurt, flour, baking powder, bicarbonate of soda and salt to the bowl. Use your hands to combine and bring it together into a sticky dough, making sure the flour is completely incorporated. Dust with a little more flour, then knead the dough and shape into a smooth ball. Cover the bowl with a clean dry tea towel and leave in a warm place for 1 hour, until doubled in size.

3   Shape the dough into 8 even balls. On a lightly dusted surface, use a rolling pin to roll out each piece of dough into an oval shape, about 20cm long and 5mm thick.

4   Heat a large frying pan over medium–high heat until very hot. Carefully coat the bottom of the pan with a small amount of melted butter. Place a flatbread in the pan, then brush its surface with a little more melted butter. Cover the pan with a lid and cook for 1 minute. When the dough has puffed up, gently turn it over and cook, lid off, for 1–2 minutes, until you can see dark spots underneath and the bread is cooked through. Wrap the cooked flatbreads in a clean tea towel to keep warm while you cook the rest.

5   Melt the remaining butter with the garlic in a small pan over low heat for 3–5 minutes, stirring until the garlic is lightly browned. Remove from the heat, stir in the herbs and drizzle over the warm flatbreads to serve.

Tips To make ahead, you can knead the dough and then leave it to prove overnight in the fridge.

Store in an airtight container at room temperature for up to 3 days or in the fridge for up to 7 days.

Leftovers are amazing: reheat in a frying pan with a little oil for about 3 minutes.

 8 breads
 15 mins
 20–30 mins
 Up to 7 days
 Up to 3 months

Non-dairy

Best Ever 'Buttermilk' Pancakes

As an American, being able to make a stack of light and fluffy pancakes for weekend breakfasts is essential! I've been perfecting this recipe for years. No need to look elsewhere for pancake recipes, this is for sure the best! Top with fruit and drizzle with maple syrup, or turn to page 170 for some alternative topping ideas.

360ml milk
2 tbsp apple cider vinegar
  or lemon juice
150g buckwheat flour
100g gluten-free plain flour
zest of 1 lemon
1½ tsp baking powder
1 tsp bicarbonate of soda
2 tsp caster sugar
½ tsp salt
1 tbsp chia seeds (optional)
1 tbsp vegetable oil, plus more
  for greasing (optional)

1   To make the 'buttermilk', whisk the milk and apple cider vinegar in a bowl until foamy and set aside for 5–10 minutes.

2   In a large mixing bowl, whisk together the flours, lemon zest, baking powder, bicarbonate of soda, sugar, salt and chia seeds, if using. Keep whisking, slowly pouring in the 'buttermilk' mixture and the oil, until the batter is smooth and pourable and the flour is completely incorporated.

3   Heat a non-stick frying pan over medium heat (depending on your pan, you may like to add a little oil to prevent the pancakes from sticking). Once the pan is hot, pour in half-ladlefuls of the batter to make small pancakes. Cook for 1–2 minutes, until the pancakes rise and bubbles appear on the surface. Carefully turn them over and cook on the other side for 1 minute. Keep warm while you cook the remaining batter.

4   To serve, stack the pancakes high and serve with fresh seasonal fruit and maple syrup.

Tips Do not flatten the pancakes with the spatula as they cook: allow them to rise to thick, fluffy pancakes.

Buckwheat flour is naturally gluten-free, but brands vary: if gluten is an issue for you, check the label. You may also need to check the label of the baking powder.

10 mins

10–15 mins

3 days

Up to
1 month

GF

12
pancakes

Cinnamon and Chocolate Churros

When I was living in New York, every day outside the subway station in Brooklyn two women sold the most incredible churros from a shopping trolley. Crispy, fried bread coated in cinnamon-and-nutmeg-spiced sugar and dunked in melted chocolate, just like those NY churros these are made with love and completely irresistible.

475ml milk (I use oat)
200g sugar, plus 3 tbsp
50ml vegetable oil, plus more
for deep frying
240g gluten-free plain flour
1 tsp baking powder
½ tsp ground ginger
1 tbsp ground cinnamon
¼ tsp ground nutmeg
150g dark chocolate,
roughly chopped

1 Pour the milk into a medium-sized saucepan over medium heat. Stir in 3 tablespoons of sugar until the sugar has dissolved. Bring to the boil, then immediately remove from the heat, stir through the oil, then stir through the flour, baking powder and ground ginger until it comes together into a dough ball. Transfer the dough to a piping bag fitted with a small star-shaped nozzle.

2 In a shallow bowl, mix the remaining sugar with the cinnamon and nutmeg.

3 Melt two-thirds of the chocolate in a heatproof bowl set over a pan of barely simmering water, ensuring the bottom of the bowl doesn't touch the water. Stir frequently until the chocolate has completely melted. Add the remaining chocolate, remove the bowl from the heat and stir until the chocolate is silky smooth.

4 To cook your churros, heat 5–7cm of vegetable oil in a large, deep heavy-based pan set over high heat until it reaches 185–190°C. I use a cook's thermometer to check the temperature. If you don't have a cook's thermometer, carefully drop in a small piece of the dough: it should immediately sizzle and turn golden brown.

5 When the oil is hot enough, carefully pipe 5–7cm lengths of dough directly into the hot oil – do not overcrowd the pan – and fry for about 1 minute, until golden brown underneath, then gently flip to cook on the other side.

6 Use a slotted spoon or tongs to transfer the cooked churros to some kitchen paper to remove excess oil. Sprinkle with the spiced sugar and toss to coat. Repeat with rest of the dough.

7 To serve, dip the hot sugar-coated churros in the melted chocolate.

Tips Check that the baking powder is gluten-free if gluten is an issue for you.

Serve immediately or they will go soft.

 8   15 mins   15 mins   **GF**

Non-dairy

Spongy Banana and Chocolate Glaze Doughnuts

Making these doughnuts is probably the best reason I know to use up old ripe bananas! Bananas bring sweetness, flavour and extra moisture to the dough, while a dark chocolate glaze provides a sophisticated finish. If you don't know about doughnut holes, be prepared to meet your new favourite bite-sized treat!

10g active dry yeast
50g plus ¼ tsp granulated sugar
60ml lukewarm water
180ml oat milk, or other non-dairy alternative
65g ripe banana, mashed
70g butter, melted and cooled
1 tsp vanilla extract
½ tsp salt
535g plain flour, plus more for dusting
vegetable oil, for frying, plus ½ tsp

Chocolate glaze
150g dark chocolate, roughly chopped

Optional toppings
crushed walnuts
toasted desiccated coconut

Tips Don't overcrowd the pan or the temperature of the oil will drop.

Drizzle the chocolate glaze over the doughnuts or dunk them in to coat them on one side.

If there's any leftover chocolate, save it or drizzle it over anything you like.

Best served hot!

1 In a small mixing bowl, whisk the yeast, ¼ teaspoon granulated sugar and warm water. Once foamy, let it stand for about 5 minutes.

2 Meanwhile, in a large mixing bowl, combine the oat milk, mashed banana, butter, vanilla extract, salt and remaining granulated sugar. Add the yeast mixture and stir well.

3 Add 40g flour at a time to the wet mixture, mixing well with a dough whisk or wooden spoon, until no streaks of flour can be seen before adding more flour. With floured hands, place the dough on a floured surface and knead lightly to form a ball. Place the ball of dough in a large bowl, and drizzle ½ teaspoon oil around the inside of the bowl. Cover with a damp clean tea towel and keep in a warm, controlled environment, like the inside of an oven, for about 1½ hours, until doubled in size.

4 Transfer the risen dough to a floured surface and lightly sprinkle with flour. With a rolling pin, gently roll the dough into a 35 x 25cm rectangle. The rectangle should be 2.5cm thick. With a doughnut cutter or a 3cm round cutter and a 1–1.5cm cutter for the holes, cut out rounds as close together as possible. Gather the leftover scraps of dough, reroll and cut again. Repeat until there's no dough remaining.

Continued $\longrightarrow$

 Makes 12–14 doughnuts, plus doughnut holes

 30 mins

 20 mins

 Up to 3 days

Up to 3 months

Continued $\longrightarrow$

5 Place the doughnuts and doughnut holes on a baking tray lined with baking parchment, making sure there's space between them to rise. Cover lightly with clingfilm and let them rise somewhere warm for 30–45 minutes until puffed up.

6 Pour the vegetable oil into a large wide, heavy-based pan to a depth of about 5cm. Heat over medium-high heat to 180°C – test it with a kitchen thermometer or drop in a small cube of bread; it should sizzle and turn brown in about 15 seconds. Meanwhile, line 2 wire racks with kitchen paper.

7 Carefully lower a few doughnuts and holes into the hot oil, making sure to not overcrowd the pan. Fry for about 2 minutes, until the golden brown underneath. Carefully flip them over once and fry for 1–2 minutes. The doughnut holes will take less time to cook, so keep a closer eye on them. Remove with a skimmer or slotted spoon and place on the wire racks to cool.

8 Place two-thirds of the chocolate in a heatproof bowl that fits over a saucepan. Bring about 2.5cm water to a simmer over medium-high heat. Set the bowl over the saucepan, making sure the bottom of the bowl doesn't touch the hot water. Reduce the heat, and melt the chocolate, stirring frequently. Once the chocolate has completely melted, add the remaining chocolate to the bowl, remove from heat and let it cool slightly, continuing to stir until the chocolate is silky smooth.

9 Once the chocolate is slightly cooled, scoop some chocolate onto a spoon and drizzle the chocolate over the tops of the doughnut rings, creating a pattern of your liking. Dip the doughnut holes in the chocolate glaze and return to the rack.

10 Sprinkle over any additional toppings while the chocolate is still slightly wet and glossy. Let the doughnuts and holes stand until the glaze sets.

Blackberry Shortbread Frozen Yoghurt

I've been trying to find a frozen yoghurt recipe that has the perfect creamy consistency but that's also quite quick to make – and this is it! It's sweet and smooth, with buttery, crunchy biscuits folded through for contrasting textures. Freeze-dried raspberries on top add extra colour and sweetness.

400g blackberries
400g yoghurt
200g sweetened condensed milk
50g maple syrup
2 tsp vanilla extract
200ml double cream
zest and juice of 1 lemon
150g shortbread biscuits or cookies, crushed and chilled in the fridge
4 tbsp freeze-dried strawberries or raspberries

1 In a food processor, blend half the blackberries with the yoghurt, condensed milk, maple syrup and vanilla extract until smooth and creamy.

2 Pour the double cream and lemon juice into a large mixing bowl and, with a hand mixer, lightly whip for about 5 minutes until it's increased in size and bubbly. Stir in the blackberry mixture and lemon zest until combined. Pour the mixture into a freezer-proof container and cover with a lid or clingfilm. Freeze for 1 hour.

3 After 1 hour, remove from the freezer and whisk until smooth. Fold through the remaining blackberries and frozen shortbread biscuits. Scatter the freeze-dried fruit on top and cover. Freeze for another hour, or overnight.

4 Remove from the freezer to soften a little before serving. Run an ice cream scoop or large spoon under hot water, wipe clean and scoop.

Tips Blackberries are the hero here, but you can swap them out for strawberries, blueberries or raspberries.

The water content of each berry may vary. Sometimes I like to press the fruit through a sieve, capturing the liquid and freezing it for smoothies and cocktails. Keep the fruit pulp and continue with the recipe. More water content means the end product will have shards of ice throughout.

You can sub lemon for orange.

Try folding through crushed cardamom pods or a drizzle of balsamic vinegar in step 3.

 8

 10 minutes

Freeze time: 2 hours or overnight

 Up to 3 months

Fluffy Scones

There's not much better than filling your home with the smell of baking. Allow these light and airy scones to cool a little before topping with a generous dollop of jam and thick cream. The only question is: which one goes on first? Definitely cream first then the jam, right?

150ml milk (I use oat)
1 tsp vanilla extract
1 tbsp lemon juice and zest of 1 lemon
300g self-raising flour, plus more
  for dusting
1 tsp baking powder
90g butter, cold and cubed
50g caster sugar

To serve
strawberry jam
thick cream

1 Heat the milk in a pan over low heat until lukewarm – keep an eye on it as you don't want it to get too hot. Remove from the heat and stir in the vanilla and lemon juice. Set aside to cool.

2 Preheat the oven to 220°C/200°C fan/gas 7. Line a baking sheet with baking parchment.

3 Sift the flour and baking powder into a large bowl. Add the butter and use your fingertips to lightly rub everything together until it looks like fine crumbs. Stir in the sugar and lemon zest.

4 Reserving 2 tablespoons of the milk mixture for brushing on top of your scones, pour the rest into the flour mixture and lightly knead for about 2 minutes, until you have a shaggy, slightly sticky dough. On a lightly floured surface, use your fingertips to gently press out the dough until it is about 3cm thick. Using a 5–8cm round cutter, cut out the scones and place them on the lined baking sheet. Gather the leftover dough, reroll and cut out more scones. You should get 8 or 9.

5 Lightly brush the scones with the reserved milk mixture and bake for 15–20 minutes, until well risen and golden brown. Remove from the oven and leave to cool on a wire rack.

6 Split the scones and serve with strawberry jam and cream.

Tips Don't overhandle the dough, and don't roll it out too thinly or you won't have deep, fluffy scones.

Store leftovers in an airtight container at room temperature for up to 3 days or in the fridge for up to 5 days.

 8 or 9 scones   20 mins   15–20 mins   Up to 5 days   Up to 1 month

No-waste Cereal Milk Ice Cream

This is based on the incredible breakfast-meets-dessert treat created by the amazing Momofuku Milk Bar in New York. When I first tried it more than ten years ago, it blew my mind – as a kid, drinking that sweetened milk at the bottom of the cereal bowl was always the best bit, and here was the adult version turned into ice cream!

75g cornflakes, or any cereal
1 x 400g tin full-fat coconut milk
200ml milk (I use oat)
1 tsp ground cinnamon
1 tsp vanilla extract
100g sweetened condensed
    coconut milk
2 tbsp sugar
1 tsp olive oil
sea salt

1 Preheat the oven to 150ºC/130ºC fan/gas 2. Line a baking sheet with baking parchment.

2 Spread the cornflakes evenly over the baking sheet and bake for 10–15 minutes, until lightly browned. Remove from the oven and leave to cool.

3 In a pan over low heat, gently stir the coconut milk and oat milk, ensuring that any solid coconut has melted. Leave to cool for 10 minutes.

4 Transfer the toasted cornflakes to a large mixing bowl and pour in the cooled coconut and oat milk, cinnamon and vanilla; stir well to combine. Leave to infuse for 30 minutes.

5 Strain the mixture through a fine sieve into another large bowl. Gently press as much milk as you can from the cornflakes: if small bits of cereal fall into the milk, this is fine. Place the used cornflakes in a small container, seal with a lid and place in the fridge.

6 Whisk the infused milk with the condensed coconut milk, half the sugar and a pinch of sea salt until well combined. Transfer the mixture to a freezer-proof container with a lid, seal and freeze overnight, until solid.

7 Shortly before serving, preheat the oven to 170°C/150°C fan/gas 3 and line a baking sheet with baking parchment.

8 In a mixing bowl, combine the used cornflakes with the olive oil and the remaining sugar. Spread the mixture evenly over the lined baking sheet and bake for 12–15 minutes until golden and lightly crispy. Remove from the oven and leave to cool. Lightly crush to break up into small clusters.

9 Remove the ice cream from the freezer and serve immediately, in a bowl, cup or cone, topped with the cornflake clusters and a pinch of salt.

 6
 15 mins
 25–30 mins
 Up to 3 months

Non-dairy

Salted Chocolate, Peanut Butter and Tahini Brownies

Have you ever seen a more psychedelic, magical brownie?! *Photo overleaf*

2 tbsp flaxseed meal
170g plain flour
60g cocoa powder
2 tsp baking powder
150g brown sugar
¼ tsp sea salt, plus more for finishing
320g dark chocolate chips
½ tsp instant coffee
230g oat milk or non-dairy alternative
120g butter, melted
1 tsp vanilla extract
50g smooth peanut butter
25g tahini

1 Preheat the oven to 200°C/180°C fan/gas 6. Line a 23 x 23cm baking tin with baking parchment.

2 In a small bowl, combine the flaxseeds with 3 tablespoons of water. Set aside for about 5–10 minutes until it thickens and develops a jelly-like consistency.

3 Into a large mixing bowl, sift the flour, cocoa powder and baking powder. Stir in the sugar and salt.

4 Place a heatproof bowl over a saucepan of simmering water, making sure the bottom of the bowl doesn't touch the hot water. Weigh out and set aside 100g of the chocolate. Melt two-thirds of the remaining chocolate in the heatproof bowl, stirring often. Once completely melted, add the remaining one-third of the chocolate and the instant coffee powder, remove from heat and stir until silky smooth. Leave to cool for 5 minutes.

5 Fold the melted chocolate, oat milk, butter, flaxseed paste and vanilla extract into the dry ingredients until well combined. Pour the mixture into the lined baking tin. Tap gently against the counter to remove any trapped air bubbles.

6 Bake for 25 minutes; the top should be slightly cracked and cooked whereas the inside should be slightly gooey. Remove from the oven and allow to cool completely in the tin.

7 Set a heatproof bowl over a pan of simmering water, making sure it doesn't touch the water. Melt two-thirds of the remaining chocolate in the bowl, stirring. Once melted, add the rest of it, remove from the heat and stir until smooth. Cool for 5 minutes.

8 Spread the remaining chocolate mixture over the brownies, top with dollops of peanut butter and tahini. Using a knife or a toothpick, gently swirl the peanut butter and tahini together to create a magical design. Transfer the brownies to the fridge to cool for about 45 minutes.

9 Cut the chilled brownies, sprinkle of sea salt and serve.

 12
 10 mins
 1 hour
Up to 3 days at room temperature; 7 days in the fridge
 Up to 1 month

Non-dairy

8– Fruits

Apple
Bananas
Berries
Citrus

Lemon and Poppy Seed Shortbread Fingers with Lemon Glaze

I can't resist a lemon-flavoured biscuit or cake. Don't get me started on lemon drizzle... In these buttery, crumbly shortbread fingers, poppyseeds provide extra crunch and a subtle flavour that goes really well with citrus fruits. A sweet lemon glaze brings everything together. Perfect with a cup of tea. Or with ice cream. Or with yoghurt for breakfast. There are no rules to eating these!

200g very cold butter
100g caster sugar
zest of 3 lemons and juice of 1 lemon
   (save the remaining lemons to make
   my Citrus Cubes page 252)
1 tbsp poppy seeds, plus more
   for decorating
1 tsp vanilla extract
300g plain flour
pinch of salt
100g icing sugar

1   Preheat the oven to 180°C/160°C fan/gas 4. Line a 20cm x 30cm baking tray with baking parchment.

2   Put the cold butter in a bowl with the sugar and use electric beaters to whip until light and fluffy. Whip in the lemon zest, poppy seeds and the vanilla extract.

3   Fold in the flour along with a pinch of salt, then tip the mixture into the prepared tin and press down a little. Use a knife to score 20 rectangles (3 x 10cm), not cutting all the way through – this makes the shortbread fingers easier to cut after baking.

4   Bake for 30 minutes, until lightly golden. Allow to cool, then cut and place on a wire rack over a plate.

5   In a small bowl, mix the icing sugar with the juice of half a lemon and stir well. Add as much of the other half of the lemon juice as you need to make a thick-drizzle icing. Drizzle the lemony glaze over the shortbread, then sprinkle with poppy seeds and leave to set.

Tip Try substituting the lemon for lime, orange or grapefruit.

 20 fingers   10 mins   30 mins   Up to 2 weeks   Up to 1 month

Blueberry Ginger Galette

The more rustic this looks, the better. Don't stress about folding the pastry perfectly, just enjoy the process. Easy to make, this fruity pud is really beautiful and sure to win over any crowd. It just needs a scoop of ice cream before serving.

220g plain flour, plus more
  for dusting
30g granulated sugar
1 tsp salt
120g cold butter, cubed
2 tbsp cold water
1 tsp lemon juice
2 tsp milk (I use oat)

Blueberry filling
300g fresh blueberries
1 tsp grated fresh ginger,
  or 1 tbsp ground ginger
zest of 1 lemon and juice of ½
50g granulated sugar
2 tsp cornflour

1 In a food processor, combine the flour, sugar and salt, then add the butter and pulse until the mixture looks like fine crumbs. Tip the mixture into a large mixing bowl, add the cold water and lemon juice and work with your hands to combine until the mixture forms a ball of dough.

2 Tip the dough onto a floured surface and shape to form a disc. Place on a large plate, cover with a clean tea towel and chill for at least 1 hour, or up to 48 hours.

3 Meanwhile, put the blueberries into the same large mixing bowl with the ginger, lemon juice and zest, sugar and cornflour. Stir to combine, then chill until you're ready to roll the pastry.

4 Preheat the oven to 180°C/160°C fan/gas 4.

5 Remove the dough from the fridge and place it on a lightly floured sheet of baking parchment. Cover with another sheet of parchment. Gently roll the dough in every direction until you have a 30–35cm round (don't worry if it's not a perfect circle). Transfer the dough to a baking sheet and lift off the top sheet of parchment.

6 Spoon the blueberry mix onto the centre of the pastry (leave the wet sugary mixture in the bowl), leaving about 4–6cm around the edges. Gently lift the edges and fold them up and over the blueberry mixture, slightly overlapping the pastry as you go. Leave a blueberry window in the centre. Gently brush the edges of the pastry with the milk mixed with 1 teaspoon of the remaining blueberry sugar mixture.

7 Bake for about 35 minutes, until the pastry is golden brown and the blueberry mixture is bubbling. Remove from the oven and leave to cool slightly before cutting and serving.

8 Serve with ice cream; try my cereal milk ice cream (page 218) – but don't get confused, this isn't breakfast.

Tip You want to make sure the pastry has chilled enough before you roll it and spoon over the blueberry mixture.

 8   15 mins   35 mins   Up to 7 days   Up to 1 month

Fruits

Passionfruit and Mango Aquafaba Meringues

Fresh fruit and meringues are always a winning combination. Aquafaba is such an amazing ingredient; from pasta (on page 240) to my chocolate cake on page 250, it's so incredibly versatile. Here, it's whipped into a cloud and baked into a crunchy, crispy, perfectly chewy meringue that melts in your mouth. I like the sharp-sweet contrast of the passionfruit and mango, but swap out the tropical fruit for strawberries, blueberries, raspberries or bananas.

375ml whipping cream
300g coconut yoghurt
2 mangoes
1 passionfruit
1 kiwi, thinly sliced with the skin on

Meringue
150ml aquafaba
120g caster sugar

To serve
60g toasted dessicated coconut flakes
6 fresh mint leaves
zest of 1 lime

Tip If you have leftover meringues, store in a sealed and lined container at room temperature for 1 week or up to 1 month in the freezer.

1   Preheat the oven to 120°C/100°C fan/gas ½. Line a baking sheet with baking parchment.

2   Drain your chickpeas and measure out the reserved liquid. Tip the liquid into a large mixing bowl. (If you have a stand mixer or electric whisk, you can save yourself the arm work!) and whisk for 15–18 minutes, adding 1–2 tablespoons of sugar every minute, until it reaches stiff peaks and the mixture is glossy and thick. (You know it's ready when you can flip the bowl over your head and nothing happens!)

3   Spoon big tablespoons of the aqaufaba mix onto the lined baking sheet; you should make about 12 large meringues. Bake for 2 hours, then turn off the oven and leave them in the oven to cool for 45 minutes. Do not open the oven door.

4   In a bowl, lightly whip the whipping cream for about 2 minutes, until slightly thickened, then fold in the coconut yoghurt. Cut the cheeks from the mangoes, and peel. Blitz the flesh from 1 mango in a high-speed blender to make a purée, and tip into a bowl. Cut the passionfruit in half and spoon the pulp into the blitzed mango. Dice the remaining mango.

5   To serve, bash up half of the meringues into big chunks and fold them through the cream and yoghurt mixture. Swirl through the mango and passionfruit purée. Press 1 slice of kiwi on the inside of each jar, then spoon the meringue mixture into each jar. Top with the mango chunks and toasted coconut flakes. Crush a little more meringue and scatter on top – you might not need all the meringues! Finish with the fresh mint and lime zest.

 6   25 mins   2 hours   Up to 7 days   Up to 1 month   GF

Strawberry Granita with Lemon Crème

Each spoonful of this summer dessert is like a dance in your mouth between the sweet crunch from the strawberry ice, the zingy citrus cream and the crumbly shortbread pieces. Eat it in a bowl or cone - or straight from the tub. I'm not here to judge.

500ml water
200g caster sugar
600g strawberries
1 tsp vanilla extract
zest and juice of 1 lemon
250ml whipping cream
2 tbsp icing sugar
shortbread, to serve (see my Lemon
 and Poppy Seed Shortbread
 on page 224)

1   Start by tipping the water and sugar into a large saucepan. Place over a medium heat, stirring occasionally for about 2 minutes, until the sugar has dissolved.

2   Blitz all the strawberries, including the stem and leaves, in a high-speed blender to make a purée.

3   Remove the saucepan from the heat and add the strawberry purée, vanilla extract and lemon juice. Stir well, then pour the mixture into a roasting tin and slide into the freezer. Every 45 minutes for the next 5–6 hours, remove the tin and use a fork to scrape and break up the ice crystals – you'll be left with a perfect granita!

4   When you're ready to serve, lightly whip the cream, lemon zest and icing sugar. Spoon the granita into bowls or glasses, top with the lemon cream and serve with shortbread.

Tip Strawberry leaves are edible, but totally optional.

 6   10 mins   2 mins   Up to 3 months

Chocolate Orange Peanut Cheesecake

Beautifully rich and chocolatey, candied orange takes this cheesecake to another dimension! It has a peanut and biscuit base, coconut cream filling and a chocolate orange topping. With layers of flavour and texture in every slice, it's a total showstopper!

Chocolate peanut base
250g gluten-free digestive biscuits
2 tbsp cocoa powder
50g peanuts, chopped
70g butter, melted and cooled
   to room temperature
1 tbsp smooth peanut butter

Orange cheesecake
600g cream cheese
zest of 2 oranges
200g full-fat coconut cream
150g icing sugar
1 tsp vanilla extract

Chocolate ganache topping
200g full-fat coconut cream
200g dark chocolate, roughly chopped
zest of 1 orange

Candied orange and peanut topping
sliced oranges (from above)
200g sugar
100ml water

To serve
3 tbsp roasted peanuts, roughly
   chopped
1 tbsp dark chocolate, shaved
any reserved orange zest

1 Start by making the peanut chocolate base. Blitz the digestives to a fine crumble in a food processor and tip into a mixing bowl. Stir together the rest of the ingredients, then use a spoon to press into the base of a 23cm springform tin.

2 Next make the orange cheesecake layer: whisk the cream cheese with the zest from the oranges, the coconut cream, icing sugar and vanilla extract. Pour the mixture into the springform tin and chill in the fridge to set for 4–5 hours, or overnight.

3 For the chocolate ganache topping, heat the coconut cream over a medium heat until bubbling. Remove from the heat and pour over the chocolate in a bowl. Allow to sit for 2 minutes before whisking together. Stir in the orange zest. Cool until you can touch it, then pour over the set cheesecake and put back in the fridge.

4 Slice the zested oranges as finely as you can, ideally 3–4mm thick. Add the sugar to a large frying pan with the water, and bring to the boil, stirring until the sugar has dissolved. Add the orange slices, turn the heat down to a simmer, and cook for 5–10 minutes, until softened and translucent. Take off the heat and allow to cool in the syrup. Use tongs to move the cool candied orange wheels to a plate lined with baking parchment or a wire rack. (You can store the candied orange slices for 3–4 weeks, in their syrup, in a jar in the fridge.)

5 Lay the slices on the top of the cheesecake, overlapping them so they fit the shape evenly. Place the cheesecake back in the fridge for another 30–45 minutes to chill.

6 To serve, slice the cheesecake and scatter with the roasted crushed peanuts, shaved chocolate and orange zest.

 8-10 45 mins 15 mins Up to 1 week Up to 1 month* (Just potatoes) **GF**

Sticky Apple Toffee Pudding

The warm, spiced cake, the sweet and sticky caramel sauce... since moving to the UK, I've become a big fan of sticky toffee pudding! Why not elevate yours by adding apples? I always serve mine with a scoop of ice cream for that irresistible hot-cold contrast.

butter, for greasing
300g Medjool dates
2½ tbsp flaxseed meal
250ml oat milk
1 tsp bicarbonate of soda
75ml water
250g self-raising flour
250ml sunflower oil
2 tbsp golden or maple syrup
150g light brown sugar
1 tsp ground cinnamon
pinch of salt
3 apples or pears (or a mixture),
  cored and cut into 1cm cubes
ice cream or cream, to serve

Sauce
100g butter
200g dark brown sugar
1 tbsp golden or maple syrup
100ml double cream

1   Preheat the oven to 180°C/160°C fan/gas 4. Line a large cake tin with baking parchment and lightly grease with butter – I used a deep 20cm brownie tin, but a 20 x 30cm tray would work as well.

2   Put the dates, flaxseed, oat milk, bicarbonate of soda and water in a saucepan over medium heat. Cook for 5 minutes, stirring occasionally, until the dates are softened. Remove from heat and allow to cool for 10 minutes.

3   Sift the flour into a large mixing bowl, then add the sunflower oil, golden syrup, sugar, cinnamon, a pinch of salt and the date mixture. Stir until combined; the batter should be quite thick.

4   Add the cubed fruit, stir to combine then tip into the prepared tin and bake for 40–45 minutes. To check it's cooked, insert a fork into the middle; it should come out clean.

5   Meanwhile, make the sauce. Melt the butter in a small saucepan over medium heat. Add the sugar and syrup, stirring slowly and continuously until the sugar has dissolved. When the sugar has completely dissolved, slowly pour in the double cream while stirring until combined and the sauce is slightly thick and shiny. Set aside ready to be reheated on a low heat when you want to serve.

6   Remove the pudding from the oven and allow it to cool for 10–15 minutes. Serve with ice cream or cream and drizzled in the sweet buttery sauce.

 8

 20 mins

 45–50 mins

 Up to 1 week

 Up to 3 months*
*Pudding only

Spiced Apple Fritters

There are few things in life that are as delicious or as comforting as a warm home-made dessert, like these fried nuggets of cinnamon-flavoured batter stuffed with juicy apple chunks and covered with a lemony drizzle. You can have these scrumptious spiced apple fritters in your hands in less than an hour.

2 large cooking apples, cored
  and cubed
2 tbsp lemon juice
2 tbsp ground flaxseed
4 tbsp water
45g butter, melted
150ml milk (I use oat)
200g plain flour
2 tsp baking powder
1 tsp ground cinnamon
½ tsp ground nutmeg
¼ tsp ground ginger
pinch of ground cardamom
½ tsp sea salt
30g sugar
1 tbsp lemon zest
vegetable oil, for deep frying
160g icing sugar

1 Toss the apples in a bowl with the lemon juice to stop them from browning. Set aside.

2 In a mixing bowl, combine the flaxseed and water, whisk together and set aside for about 5–10 minutes until it thickens. Stir in the melted butter and milk until combined.

3 Sift the flour, baking powder, spices and salt into a large bowl. Add the sugar and lemon zest, then pour in the wet mixture and stir well to create a thick batter. Add the apples to the batter, reserving the lemon juice. Mix to combine, then place the batter in the fridge for 20–30 minutes.

4 Pour 5–7cm of vegetable oil into a large, wide pan and place over medium–high heat until the oil reaches 180°C. I use a cook's thermometer to check the temperature; if you don't have one, carefully drop in a small amount of batter: it should immediately sizzle and turn golden brown.

5 Once the oil is hot, add the batter, a heaped dessertspoon at a time – do not overcrowd the pan. Fry undisturbed for 1–2 minutes, then carefully flip and fry the other side until the fritters to cool for 10–15 minutes.

6 Meanwhile, in a bowl, whisk the icing sugar with the reserved lemon juice until it's slightly thickened and glossy. Pour over the fritters; leave to set for a few minutes before serving.

Tips Any apple (or pear) will work just fine

Don't make the fritters too big, or the middle may not cook through.

 12–14 fritters   20 mins   15 mins   Up to 5 days   Up to 1 month

Banoffee Moon Pies

Moon pies are such a nostalgic recipe for me. Down the street from my school was a bakery that produced cakes, cookies, doughnuts and moon pies in a giant warehouse to sell across the US. You could smell the melting sugar in the air. In these grown-up versions, crumbly peanut cookies sandwich sticky marshmallow and banana, then they are coated in chocolate. You'll start with a full moon, then quickly have a total lunar eclipse when you eat the whole thing.

300g dark chocolate
2 ripe bananas (save the peel to make my BLT on page 241)

Peanut butter biscuits
100g butter
100g smooth peanut butter
80g caster sugar
300g plain flour, plus more for dusting
pinch of salt
3–4 tbsp cold milk, if needed
  (I use oat milk)

Marshmallow fluff
150ml aquafaba
1 tsp cream of tartar
150g caster sugar
2 tsp vanilla extract

1 Add the butter and peanut butter to a stand mixer with a paddle attachment (or you can do this by hand or use a hand whisk). Beat until light and fluffy. Add the sugar and beat again until creamy and light. Stir in the flour along with a pinch of salt. If the batter is too thick and floury add 1 tablespoon of cold milk at a time to loosen it.

2 Lay a piece of clingfilm or baking parchment along your work surface, tip the mixture onto the clingfilm and bring together. Wrap in clingfilm or baking parchment in a big flat disc, and place in the fridge to chill and firm up for 1 hour.

3 Preheat the oven to 180°C/160°C fan/gas 4. Line a baking sheet with baking parchment.

4 Lightly flour a surface and roll out the dough to 5mm thickness. Use a small glass or a 4cm or 5cm cookie cutter to cut out biscuits from the dough. Use a spatula or palette knife to lift the biscuits onto the lined tray. Combine any leftover dough and repeat until there's no dough left.

5 Bake for 10–12 minutes, until golden brown (you may have to do this in batches or over a couple of trays). Cool on a wire rack. If the biscuits are soft, allow to cool on the baking sheet before transferring.

20
moon pies

45 mins

10–12 mins

Up to 1 week

❄ Up to 1 month

6 While they are cooling, make the marshmallow fluff. Drain the chickpeas (use the chickpeas for my Curried Pumpkin and Chickpeas on 120). Measure out the liquid and tip into the bowl of a stand mixer with the whisk attachment (or a use a hand whisk). Add the cream of tartar and whisk until stiff peaks from, then add the sugar a spoonful at a time, continuing to whisk for about 15 minutes, until thick and glossy. Add the vanilla extract and give it a final whisk, then transfer to a piping bag if you have one. Keep in the fridge to cool.

7 Melt two-thirds of the chocolate in a heatproof bowl set over a pan of simmering water. Make sure the bottom of the bowl doesn't touch the hot water. Add the remaining one-third of chocolate and stir until smooth and shiny.

8 Assembly time! Pipe the marshmallow fluff over half of the biscuits on the rack, using around 1–2 teaspoon on each. Slice the bananas and place on top of the marshmallow fluff. Top with the other half of the biscuits to create little sandwiches. Dip the biscuit sandwiches in the melted chocolate so they're well coated. Set aside on a wire rack before placing in the fridge to set the chocolate.

8- Leftovers

Fresh No-egg Pasta

This pasta is made without eggs: it uses aquafaba from a tin of chickpeas. I make this recipe every Friday night ('pasta night'!), so if it's Friday night for you, let's make it together!

100g 00 flour, plus more for dusting
50ml aquafaba
⅛ tsp ground turmeric

1   Pour the flour onto a clean worktop, and create a small well in the middle. Add the aquafaba and turmeric to the centre of the well. Using your fingers, combine them into the flour until you have a shaggy ball of dough. Knead for about 5–10 minutes, until the dough is smooth.

2   Alternatively, add the flour and turmeric to a stand mixer; on a low speed, pour in the aquafaba and mix until you have a rough ball of dough. Tip out onto a floured worktop and knead for 5–10 minutes until the dough is smooth.

3   Wrap the dough in clingfilm or baking parchment and set aside for 15 minutes. This will help the pasta stretch.

4   When you're ready to roll, lightly flour the dough as needed. Pass the dough through a pasta machine, starting at its widest setting. Decrease the setting by one notch and pass the dough through again. Repeat, passing the dough through each setting once.

5   Alternatively, gently roll the dough with a long rolling pin. Lightly flour the dough when needed.

6   To make spaghetti or tagliatelle, cut the pasta with a long, sharp knife or pass it through the machine. Gather the pasta and place it on a baking sheet; leave to rest for 5 minutes.

7   Bring a large pan of salted water to the boil, add the pasta and cook, stirring occasionally, for about 2 minutes. Strain the pasta and serve with my Simplest Tomato Sauce (page 00).

Tips If making 2 or more portions, you will need to divide the dough, working with 1 portion at a time. Keep any unrolled dough under a clean damp tea towel to prevent it from drying out.

Swap aquafaba for the liquid from a tin of cannellini or red kidney beans.

Use a pasta maker for perfectly rolled pasta dough.

Great for making ravioli, spaghetti or wider noodles.

Make ahead: keep the dough wrapped in the fridge for up to 2 days.

 1   25 mins   2 mins   Up to 3 days   Up to 1 month

BLT

The B stands for banana skin! Now I'm not going to force you to eat banana skins, but if there was ever a time to try them, this would be that moment. Bananas are one of the most-wasted fruits in the world. In the UK, over 1 million bananas go to waste every day. Don't slip on this recipe. Crispy, smoky banana skins are my winner over bacon, any day! *Photo overleaf*

4 ripe bananas
2 tbsp soy sauce or tamari
2 tsp brown sugar
1 tsp smoked paprika
½ tsp garlic powder
½ tsp liquid smoke (optional)
1 tbsp vegetable oil
4 slices white bread, toasted
8 lettuce leaves
2 heirloom tomatoes, sliced 5mm thick

Maple miso mustard
2 tbsp mustard
2 tsp maple syrup
1 tsp miso
¼ tsp cayenne pepper
salt

Lemon-herb mayonaise
4 tbsp mayonnaise
1 small garlic clove, finely grated
1 tbsp lemon juice
1 tsp lemon zest
2 tbsp freshly chopped mixed herbs
  (e.g. basil, parsley, chives, dill)
black pepper

Tip For a gluten-free version, use tamari and gluten-free bread.

1 Wash the bananas very well. Remove the skin, and slice the banana and keep in the freezer for a smoothie later. Cut both ends off the skin. Using a spoon, scrape off the fleshy part inside, then cut each piece of skin into 3 strips.

2 In a shallow bowl, whisk together the soy sauce, brown sugar, smoked paprika, garlic powder and liquid smoke, if using. Add the banana skins, turn to coat in the marinade and leave for about 15 minutes.

3 Preheat the oven to 190°C/170°C fan/gas 5. Line a baking sheet with baking parchment.

4 Heat the oil in a large non-stick frying pan over medium heat. Add a few slices of the marinated skins, outer side down first. Cook for 1–2 minutes until crispy around the edges, then flip and cook the other side for 1–2 minutes. Transfer the cooked banana skins to the lined baking sheet. Repeat until you have fried all the banana skins.

5 Brush with the remaining marinade, then cook in the oven for 5–6 minutes, flipping halfway, until crispy. Transfer to a wire rack to cool slightly.

6 Meanwhile, make the maple miso mustard. Whisk the mustard with the maple syrup, miso, cayenne and a pinch of salt until combined. Set aside.

7 For the lemon-herb mayonnaise, stir together the mayonnaise, garlic, lemon juice and zest, mixed herbs and a pinch of salt and black pepper.

8 To serve, spread 2 pieces of toast with the lemon-herb mayo and add 4 lettuce leaves on each. Top with the banana skin 'bacon' and the tomato slices. Spread the remaining slices of toast with some maple miso mustard and close the lid of the sandwich. Serve immediately.

Best Festive Leftover Sandwich

When the festive season rolls around, I'm thinking about two things: what can be saved as leftovers and how to cook up those leftovers in a creative way. This recipe gives your festive leftovers a crunchy kick. Totally drool-worthy.

4 tbsp mayonnaise
2 tsp wholegrain mustard
50g leftover Buttery Herb Stuffing (see page 74)
leftover cooked vegetables (I used roasted carrots and beetroot)
1 portion of Roast Dinner Tart (page 119) or Nut Roast Cake (page 70)
3 slices bread
1 tbsp cranberry sauce

1 Preheat the oven to 150°C/130°C fan/gas 2.

2 Mix the mayonnaise with the mustard and set aside.

3 Warm the leftovers (stuffing, vegetables, nut roast cake/roast dinner tart) in the oven for about 15 minutes.

4 Toast the bread to your desired toastiness. Spread a thin layer of cranberry sauce on 1 slice, and the mustard-mayonnaise on the other 2 slices.

5 Beginning with the first slice of bread with mustard-mayonnaise, add a layer of nut roast cake/roast dinner tart. Add the slice of bread with cranberry sauce and top with the stuffing and veg. Cover with the last slice of bread, mustard-mayo side facing down.

6 Serve immediately, and if there's any leftover gravy, don't be afraid to dip that sandwich in!

Tip Use any leftover cooked veg: beetroot, Brussels sprouts, carrots, parsnips, roast potatoes, sweet potatoes...

 1   5 mins   15 mins   Up to 5 days

Leftover Stuffing Stuffed Mushrooms

The holidays are one of the most wasteful times of the year, and so this is a great way to use up any of the super delicious leftover stuffing from page 74. These stuffed mushrooms make the ideal fun appetiser or finger food to carry on the festivities.

20 small chestnut mushrooms
zest and juice of 1 lemon
1 tbsp butter
1 small shallot, finely chopped
3 garlic cloves, finely chopped
¼ tsp dried thyme
small bunch of fresh parsley, leaves
  and stems chopped separately,
  plus more leaves to garnish
150g leftover Buttery Herb Stuffing
  (page 74)
1 tbsp extra-virgin olive oil
salt and black pepper

1 Wipe the mushrooms clean with kitchen paper. Remove the stems, leaving the mushrooms with a hollow centre. Roughly chop the stems and set aside.

2 Preheat the oven to 200°C/180°C fan/gas 6.

3 In a frying pan over medium heat, dry fry half of the mushroom caps, gills-side up, for 2 minutes. Add 1 tablespoon of lemon juice and a generous pinch of black pepper and cook for 1–2 minutes, stirring often but gently, so you don't break the caps. Transfer the caps to a plate and repeat with the second batch of mushrooms, also adding them to the plate.

4 Melt the butter in the frying pan and fry the shallot, garlic, dried thyme and 2 tablespoons of chopped parsley stems for about 4 minutes, until soft. Add the chopped mushroom stems and the juice of half the lemon and cook for about 5 minutes, stirring often.

5 Put the mushroom stem mixture into a food processor, add the parsley leaves and blitz to a purée. Tip the mixture to a bowl and combine with the leftover stuffing. Season to taste with salt and black pepper.

6 Stuff the mushroom caps with the filling and smooth over the tops. Arrange the mushroom caps close together in a baking dish. Drizzle over the extra-virgin olive oil and bake for 10–15 minutes.

7 Best served hot. To serve, garnish each mushroom with a little lemon zest and a parsley leaf.

Tips Fry the mushrooms for just a few minutes to reduce moisture and prevent them from going soggy.

Defrost, then reheat in the oven at 150°C/130°C fan/gas 2 for 10-15 minutes.

 8
 20 mins
 25–30 mins
 Up to 5 days
 Up to 2 weeks

Leftover Burger Flatbreads

Leftover burgers never tasted so good. With inspiration from Middle Eastern cooking, these burger balls are fried until crispy and sit on a pile of spicy cucumber and feta salad, with a sweet and tangy tahini sauce. Eat with a fork and knife, or get your hands involved, fold up the flatbread and take a big bite. An easy weeknight dinner or weekend brunch.

4 uncooked burger patties (page 68 or page 131)
2 tbsp freshly chopped dill, including stems
2 tbsp freshly chopped parsley, including stems
2 garlic cloves, grated
5 tbsp vegetable oil
4 flatbreads, warmed
Pickled Red Onion (page 267)
pinch of sumac (optional), to serve

Cucumber salad
1 small cucumber, peeled lengthways into ribbons
4 cherry tomatoes, chopped
1 tsp freshly chopped dill
¼ tsp ground cumin
¼ tsp smoked paprika
30g feta, crumbled
1 tbsp extra-virgin olive oil
juice of ½ lemon

Tahini sauce
100g tahini
juice of ½ lemon
1 garlic clove, finely grated
1 tsp maple syrup
1 tsp chilli paste (e.g. harissa), or to taste

1   In a mixing bowl, combine the uncooked burgers with the dill, parsley and garlic. In the palms of your hands, roll the mixture into about 20 walnut-sized balls. Place on a lined baking sheet and chill for 15 minutes.

2   To make the cucumber salad, put the cucumber in a mixing bowl, add all the remaining ingredients and toss to combine. Set aside.

3   To make the tahini sauce, put all the ingredients in a small bowl and stir until smooth. If you like things hotter, add more chilli paste.

4   Heat the vegetable oil in a frying pan over medium–high heat. Once hot, add the burger balls and fry for about 5–7 minutes, turning occasionally, until crispy. Drain on kitchen paper or a wire rack.

5   Add the cucumber salad to the warm flatbreads and top with the burger balls and pickled red onion. Drizzle with the tahini sauce and a pinch of sumac, if you like.

Tip Super-versatile: use any leftover uncooked burger.

 4
 20 mins
 10 mins
 Up to 5 days
 Up to 1 month* *burger only

Coffee Ground Pancakes

A fan favourite, with over 3 million views. The coffee grounds (depending on the variety) offer nutty, chocolatey notes and are quite subtle. Now you can drink and eat your coffee at the same time!

200g self-raising flour
1 tsp baking powder
½ tsp ground cinnamon
1 tbsp light brown sugar
30g (about 2–3 tbsp) used
  coffee grounds
300ml oat milk
2–3 tsp vegetable oil (optional)
salt

To serve
fresh strawberries
chocolate shavings
icing sugar
maple syrup

1   In a large mixing bowl, whisk together the flour, baking powder, cinnamon, sugar, coffee grounds and a pinch of salt. Keep whisking while you slowly pour in the milk, until you have a thick, pourable batter.

2   Heat a non-stick frying pan over medium heat (depending on your pan, you may like to add a little oil to prevent the pancakes from sticking). Once the pan is hot, add half-ladlefuls of the batter to make small pancakes. Cook for about 2 minutes, until the underside is golden brown and the edges are set and bubbles start to form on the surface. Flip and cook on the other side for 1–2 minutes. Keep warm while you cook the remaining batter.

3   To serve, stack the pancakes and serve with fresh strawberries, chocolate shavings, a dusting of icing sugar and maple syrup.

Tips You can also use coffee grounds in cookies, muffins or cakes.

Use gluten-free self-raising flour and baking powder if you prefer.

 12 pancakes
 5 mins
 10–15 mins
 Up to 3 days
 Up to 1 month

Triple Chocolate Birthday Cake

You'll be finding ways to use up chickpeas just so you can make this chocolate cake! Aquafaba is whisked until fluffy, then folded through chocolate and flour to produce a beautifully light cake that melts in your mouth.

150ml aquafaba
120g brown sugar
150g granulated sugar
1 tsp salt
100g butter, at room temperature
250g plain flour
85g cocoa powder
1 tsp baking powder
100ml milk

Chocolate frosting
200g dark chocolate, roughly chopped
1 tsp vanilla extract
100g full-fat coconut cream
   (from the top of a tin of coconut milk)
2 tbsp cold butter
120g icing sugar, plus a little more
   if needed
chocolate shavings, to decorate

Tips Be patient, don't rush the steps.

Incorporate fresh or freeze-dried raspberries into this cake.

1   Preheat the oven to 200°C/180°C fan/gas 6. Line two 18cm cake tins with baking parchment.

2   In a bowl, with a hand mixer, whisk the aquafaba on high-speed for 5 minutes, until foamy. Keep whisking for about 15 minutes, adding 1–2 tablespoons brown sugar every minute until glossy and stiff peaks form.

3   In a separate bowl, mix the granulated sugar, salt and butter until pale and fluffy. Sift in the flour, cocoa powder and baking powder, and fold together well. Add the milk and stir to combine. Carefully pour in the aquafaba mixture making sure not to knock out all the air and fold it in very gently.

4   Divide the cake batter between the prepared tins and bake for 30 minutes. When cooked, allow the cakes to cool in their tins for about 15 minutes. Gently release the cakes from their tins, transfer to a cooling rack and leave to cool completely.

5   To make chocolate frosting, melt two-thirds of chocolate in a heatproof bowl that fits over a saucepan of simmering water, making sure the bottom of the bowl doesn't touch the hot water, stirring occasionally. Once melted, remove from heat, and stir in the remaining one-third of the chocolate. Set aside to cool for 5 minutes.

6   In a stand mixer or by hand, mix the melted chocolate and vanilla extract on low speed, and gradually mix in the full-fat coconut cream and butter until smooth.

7   Add the icing sugar about 1–2 tablespoons at a time. The texture should be firm, soft and spreadable. Chill the frosting in the fridge for 20 minutes.

8   Once chilled, give it a quick stir. If too loose, add 1–2 tablespoons more icing sugar until firm and spreadable.

9   Spread the chocolate frosting, about 2cm thick, on top of one cake. Stack the second cake on top and spread the remaining icing on top. Finish with the shaved chocolate.

 8

 30 mins

 45 mins

1–2 days at room temperature, Up to 5 days in the fridge

 Up to 1 month

Citrus Cubes

These citrus ice cubes pack a big punch of flavour – a great way to use that last lemon or lime. Add them to a pitcher of water on a hot day for a refreshing lemon-infused drink, or add to iced tea, lemonade, smoothies or cocktails. Always good to have in the freezer during the warmer months.

1 lemon or lime
250ml water

1   Soak the fruit in warm salted water, then scrub.

2   Slice the fruit in half and remove the pips. Place the fruit in a high-speed blender, add the water and blend on high speed until smooth.

3   Pour the liquid into an ice cube tray and freeze for 4 hours or overnight.

Tip Take your citrus ice cubes to new levels by adding fresh mint leaves before freezing.

10–14 ice cubes	5 mins	❄ Up to 3 months	**GF**

Lime Tart with Candied Lime Peel

This tart is all about the candied peel! You can use any citrus you like: lemon lime, orange, blood orange, grapefruit. I love how it uses up the whole fruit with zero waste. The tart has a beautiful crumbly shortbread base with a creamy, zesty filling and a final flourish of sugary crunch on top.

85g butter
250g ginger nuts or a variety
   of shortbread biscuit
5 limes
300g block silken tofu
210g sweetened condensed milk
2 tbsp cornflour
4 tbsp icing sugar
100g caster sugar
50ml water
250ml whipping cream, to serve

1 Preheat the oven to 180°C/160°C fan/gas 4.

2 Melt the butter in a small saucepan over medium heat. Blitz the ginger nuts in a food processor, then pour in the melted butter and pulse until combined. Transfer the crumbly mixture to a 20cm tart case and press up the sides. Bake for 8–10 minutes while you prep the filling.

3 For the filling, blitz the zest and juice of 3 limes with the silken tofu, condensed milk, cornflour and 2 tablespoons of the icing sugar until smooth and creamy. Spoon into the tart case, spread and smooth evenly, and bake for 40–50 minutes, until set and the crust is golden brown. Set aside to cool completely, then refrigerate for 2–3 hours, until the filling is cold and has set.

4 While the tart is cooling, make the candied lime peel. Take the peel from the 2 un-zested limes and thinly slice into strips, or thinly slice the entire limes. Put the caster sugar and water in a small saucepan over medium heat and stir occasionally until the sugar has dissolved. Bring to a boil, then add the lime peel or slices, cook for 5 minutes, then remove from heat. With tongs, remove the lime peel or slices and lay on a wire rack to cool completely.

5 To serve, whip the cream and remaining icing sugar until thick and glossy. Pile the whipped cream in middle of the tart leaving a 2cm border all the way round. Scatter the candied lime peel into the border, then slice and serve.

Tips If you fancy really showing off, whip up some aquafaba meringue (see the Moon Pies recipe on page 236), mound it on top and blow torch to caramelise it just before serving.

Freeze for 1 month without the cream and candied peel. Candied peel can keep for up to 2 weeks in an airtight container lined with parchment paper.

 12

 20 mins

55 mins- 1 hour 5 mins

 Up to 1 week

 Up to 1 month

14 Quick Recipe Hacks

Transform and enhance any dish with these flavourful additions.

Roasted Chickpeas

These are great for adding bulk to all kinds of dishes – and they also make an irresistible snack!

1 x 400g tin chickpeas, drained and rinsed
1 tbsp olive oil
½ tsp smoked paprika
salt and black pepper

1   Preheat the oven to 220°C/200°C fan/gas 7. Line a baking tray with baking parchment.

2   Dry the chickpeas thoroughly on a clean tea towel, then toss with the oil, smoked paprika and a pinch of salt and black pepper.

3   Spread the chickpeas on the lined baking tray and roast in the oven for 10–15 minutes, tossing halfway, until golden brown and crispy.

Tip Instead of olive oil, for extra flavour use the oil from a jar of sundried tomatoes.

Chickpea Mayo

Yes, you can buy ready-made vegan mayo, but even the best brands can't compare with this easy, additive-free, home-made version. Great in sandwiches and burgers, or in dips and dressings.

3 tbsp aquafaba
1 tbsp fresh lemon juice
1 tsp apple cider vinegar
1 tsp maple syrup
½ tsp salt
140ml extra-virgin olive oil

1   In a tall container, add the aquafaba, lemon juice, vinegar, maple syrup and salt. Using a hand blender, blend to combine.

2   While blending, slowly stream in the olive oil until the mixture starts to thicken and turn pale and creamy, about 1–2 minutes.

3   Keep in a sealed container or jar in the fridge for up to 2 weeks.

Tip For additional flavour, add 1 teaspoon smoked paprika, 1 tablespoon tomato purée and 1 tablespoon harissa.

Veg Scraps Stock

Save yourself time and money and use peelings and trimmings to make delicious, vibrant veg stock. There's no turning back to using store-bought stock once you start. Use it in soups, such as my Rich Ribollita (page 75), or in any sauce or gravy.

onion scraps
garlic scraps
carrot scraps
celery scraps
herb scraps
mushroom scraps
1 bay leaf
pinch of salt

1 Put your collected scraps in a large saucepan, add the bay leaf and salt. Pour in enough water to cover the scraps.

2 Bring to the boil, then simmer for at least 10–15 minutes. Simmer longer for more flavour. You'll know it's ready when the vegetables are soft and the liquid turns a slightly darker gold colour.

3 Strain over a jug or bowl to collect the stock. Leave to cool before filling containers.

4 Keep in a sealed container in the fridge for up to 7 days or freeze for up to 3 months.

Tips Freeze peel and scraps after cooking your meals. Collect in the freezer until you have enough to make stock: a large handful of scraps will be enough to make about 1 litre of stock.

Add a few peppercorns if you like.

Don't use beetroot scraps: the colour will dominate your soups and sauces.

Don't use cabbage, broccoli or cauliflower scraps, or the stems of peppers or aubergines, or the stock will taste bitter.

DGS (Delicious Green Sauce)

This versatile bright, fresh green sauce is perfect tossed through grilled or steamed vegetables or spooned over grilled or pan-fried tofu. Any combination of soft green herbs or bagged salad will work, just be aware the flavour will change a little depending on what you use. Feel free to swap the lemon for lime or shallot for garlic to mix things up too.

handful of fresh basil, including the stems
handful of fresh parsley, including the stems
handful of fresh dill
handful of fresh chives
3 garlic cloves
60g yoghurt (I use coconut yoghurt) or sour cream
zest of 1 lemon
5 tbsp olive oil
¼ tsp salt

1 In a food processor, blitz the herbs and garlic to a paste, scraping down the sides of the processor if necessary.

2 Add the yoghurt and lemon zest and blend until smooth. With the motor running, stream in the olive oil until evenly combined. Season with the salt.

3 Use immediately or keep in a jar in the fridge for up to 3 days, covered with a thin layer of oil to preserve.

Peanut Sauce

Drizzle over noodles, salads, stir-fried veg or rice bowls.

2 tbsp peanut butter, smooth or crunchy
2 tbsp soy sauce or tamari
3 tbsp lime juice or rice vinegar
½ tsp chilli flakes
¼ tsp maple syrup
2 tbsp water

1 Put all the ingredients (except the water) into a small jar or bowl; close the lid and shake vigorously, or whisk until evenly mixed. If too thick, add a splash of water to loosen.

2 Keep in a covered container in the fridge for up to 2 weeks.

Tip For extra flavour, add 1 grated garlic clove, 1 teaspoon grated ginger and/or 1 teaspoon toasted sesame seeds.

Everything Seasoning

Sprinkle over avocado toast, hummus, roasted veggies or baked potatoes.

2 tbsp poppy seeds
1 tbsp black sesame seeds
1 tbsp white sesame seeds
1 tbsp dried minced garlic
1 tbsp dried minced onion
1 tsp dried oregano
1 tsp flaky sea salt

1 Put all the ingredients into a jar or container, close the lid and shake.

2 Store in a cool, dry cupboard for up to 6 months.

Herby Lime Salsa

A zingy salsa to serve with tacos, crisp cucumber salad, roasted veg, Crispy Smashed Potatoes (page 36) or a tofu noodle bowl such as Sticky Broccoli and Crispy Tofu (page 145).

zest of 3 limes
2 tbsp lime juice
2 garlic cloves, roughly chopped
15g fresh ginger, grated
10g fresh basil, including stems
10g fresh coriander, including stems
5g fresh mint leaves
60ml olive oil
1 tsp salt

1 In a food processor, blitz all the ingredients until you have a bright green paste, scraping down the sides of the processor if necessary.

2 Keep in a sealed jar in the fridge for up to 1 week.

Max's Go-to Salad Dressing

This works brilliantly with any salad, from simple lettuce leaves to leftover treasures such as beetroot, carrot, thinly sliced Brussels sprouts, mixed beans – all things salad. Perfect for in-a-pinch situations.

6 tbsp extra virgin olive oil
1 tsp Dijon mustard
1 tsp wholegrain mustard
1 tbsp finely chopped fresh parsley
juice of ½ lemon
2 tsp maple syrup
¼ tsp black pepper

1 Put all the ingredients into a small jar, close the lid and shake vigorously until smooth.

2 Keep in the fridge for up to 1 week.

Quick Garlic Chilli Oil

Serve with nachos, or drizzle over pizza or noodle dishes such as Quick Chilli Garlic Ramen (page 194).

80ml vegetable oil
5 garlic cloves, finely chopped
3 tsp chilli flakes
1 tsp sugar
½ tsp salt
1½ tbsp apple cider vinegar

1 Put all the ingredients into a pan over medium heat and cook for 3–4 minutes, stirring often, until bubbles start to form; reduce the heat to low and cook until the garlic is fragrant. Leave to cool slightly before pouring into a jar.

2 When cool, add a thin layer of oil (about 1 tablespoon) on top of the sauce. Keep in the fridge for up to 2 weeks.

14 Quick Recipe Hacks

Coffee Cubes

Add to your iced coffee for an extra shot or, for the perfect morning smoothie, add 2-3 coffee cubes to a blender, add 1 ripe banana and a scoop of peanut butter and top up with milk; blend until smooth.

1   Fill an ice cube tray with the last drops of coffee from your pot. Freeze overnight.

2   Keep in the freezer for up to 3 months.

Pickled Red Onion

The onion turns a bright pink shade and makes the perfect topping for curries, spiced lentils, burgers or tacos.

½ red onion, thinly sliced
3 tbsp white wine vinegar
1 tbsp granulated sugar
pinch of salt

1   Put all the ingredients in a small bowl and gently mix; set aside for at least 15 minutes.

2   Keep in a sealed container in the fridge for up to 5 days.

Green Stock Cubes

Fun fact - you can freeze herbs! Preserve the intense flavours for months and easily add them into recipes.

large bunch of any leftover leafy
   green and/or fresh herb
1–2 garlic cloves
   and/or 1–2 tbsp grated fresh ginger

1   Put your herbs and/or leafy greens in a large bowl and cover with boiling water for 30 seconds. Once they are bright green, drain the greens, then cover with cold water from the tap and leave for 1–2 minutes.

2   Drain the greens and/or herbs and place them in a blender or food processor. Add the garlic and/or ginger. Blend until you have a smooth green purée. You may need to add a little water to keep it smooth.

3   Pour the purée into an ice cube tray and freeze overnight.

Tip   Use the green cubes in any dish from stir-fries and fried rice to soups and stews. Try them in my Easy Spinach and Chickpea Curry (page 159) and Creamy Leek and Parsnip Soup (page 22).

Hot Fudge Sauce

Pour this fudge sauce over brownies, cakes, cookies and ice cream.

110g full-fat coconut cream
60g dark chocolate, roughly chopped
½ tsp vanilla extract
2 tbsp maple syrup
2 tbsp unsweetened cocoa powder
½ tsp salt

1 In a small pan over low heat, combine the coconut cream, two-thirds of the chocolate, vanilla extract and maple syrup. Stir until the chocolate melts, taking care not to burn the chocolate.

2 When the chocolate has melted, remove from the heat and whisk in the remaining chocolate, cocoa powder and salt until no lumps or streaks of powder remain and the sauce is smooth. Serve warm.

Tip Keep any leftover hot fudge sauce in a sealed jar in the fridge for up to 2 weeks. Reheat in a small pan over low heat, stirring often, until warmed through.

Blueberry Compote

A great way to jazz up your morning porridge or toast, or serve with yoghurt, ice cream, pancakes, waffles, muffins, scones –anything goes with this quick jam.

190g fresh blueberries
zest of 1 lemon
2 tsp sugar

1 Put all the ingredients into a pan over medium–low heat. Crush some of the blueberries with the back of a spoon or fork, then simmer for 5–10 minutes over low heat.

2 Remove from the heat and let it stand for 5–10 minutes. The compote will thicken slightly as it cools.

3 To serve warm, reheat in a small pan over low heat, stirring occasionally, until warmed through.

4 Keep in a sealed container in the fridge for up to 7 days or freeze for up to 3 months.

Tips Swap blueberries for raspberries or strawberries.

Swap lemon zest for orange.

How to Get the Best Out of Your Food!

Storing food properly and avoiding waste can save you time and money.

	How to Store	**How to Prep to Avoid Waste**
Potatoes	• Cool, dark, dry, well-ventilated place, away from appliances that generate heat. • Don't refrigerate. • Keep separate from onions, garlic, bananas and apples.	• Scrub; no need to peel. If you're a peeler, bake the skins to make crisps. • If sprouting, remove sprouts; cut off small green bits, but if very green, compost.
Beetroot, carrots, parsnips, celeriac, swedes, turnips	• Remove green tops and store separately. • Refrigerate root veg in a reusable bag, in the bottom drawer.	• Scrub; no need to peel. • If soft, submerge in ice-cold water for 30 minutes to bring them back to life. • If the green tops are attached, remove them and wash to remove any dirt. Sauté the greens or make pesto.
Onions	• Cool, dark, dry, well-ventilated place, away from appliances that generate heat. • Don't refrigerate. Never store in plastic bags or airtight containers. • Keep separate from potatoes.	• Thinly slice off the top, but keep the root on. Cut in half from top to bottom. Peel the skin, then slice or chop down to the root. • Once chopped, refrigerate in a sealed container or wrapped in reusable plastic.
Garlic	• Store as for onions.	• To peel easily, place cloves of garlic in a jar, seal the lid and shake vigorously for 5 seconds. The skin should fall off with a little help. • Use the entire clove, unless it's sprouting, in which case remove the green shoot.
Leeks, spring onions	• Refrigerate leeks in the bottom drawer. • Put spring onions in a jar with their roots in water; refrigerate, changing the water every other day.	• Don't throw away the green parts: they're edible. Thinly slice the green part and sauté. Slice the white part as close as you can to the root. Compost roots.
Tomatoes	• Room temperature, out of direct sunlight. • Store stem side down while they finish ripening. • Once ripe, use immediately, or keep in the fridge for a few days.	• Remove green stem, use everything else.

	How to Store	How to Prep to Avoid Waste
Aubergines	• Cool place, out of direct sunlight. Don't refrigerate. • Do not store in plastic. • Keep away from bananas, tomatoes and melons.	• Remove green stem and compost. • Once sliced or chopped, instead of sprinkling salt to extract water/reduce bitterness, place the chopped aubergine in water and soak for 20 minutes. Take a handful of the aubergine and squeeze to remove excess water. The aubergine should be soft and ready to cook.
Peppers	• Refrigerate in the bottom drawer.	• Press the green stem until it breaks the skin, then remove. There's no need to remove the top third of the peppers. • Cut in half and remove seeds, then slice or chop. • Once cut, store in an airtight container in the fridge.
Courgettes	• Keep dry: don't wash until you're ready to use. • If not used within three days, store in a paper bag with one end open to encourage ventilation, for up to two weeks. Refrigerate in the bottom drawer. • Blanch and freeze.	• The entire courgette is edible (including the flower is available). The stem is soft once cooked.
Winter squash (pumpkin, butternut squash, acorn, kabocha)	• These thick-skinned gourds can stay fresh and firm for months. Store in a cool, dry spot, out of direct sunlight. • Keep away from bananas, apples and onions.	• Scrub; no need to peel. • Get as close as you can to the stem and root, slice them off and compost. • Scoop out seeds, rinse in a bowl of water to remove pulp, pat dry and bake the seeds. • Once cut, store flesh in an airtight container in the fridge.
Cucumber	• Refrigerate uncut in the bottom drawer for up to two weeks. • Wrap cut cucumbers tightly in reusable plastic.	• I never peel cucumbers, but if you do you can use the peel to infuse water, a fruity drink or cocktail. • Wash, then slice off the hard stem and compost
Celery	• Refrigerate in the bottom drawer • Submerge cut stalks in water in a sealed glass jar.	• Use the stalks and leaves. Slice off the bottom close to the root and compost.

How to Get the Best Out of Your Food!

	How to Store	How to Prep to Avoid Waste
Cabbage, broccoli, cauliflower	• Uncut heads can be refrigerated without a bag • Once cut, store in an airtight container • Blanch and freeze.	• Leaves, florets, cores and stems are all good to eat. • If the outer part of the broccoli stem is tough, peel a little bit with a Y peeler or knife to get to the sweet, tender core; slice and cook as you would the florets. • Slice cabbage and cauliflower cores and cook with the florets. • Slice cauliflower leaves and add to a stir-fry or stew.
Leafy greens (kale, spinach, Swiss chard, salad leaves)	• Don't wash until you're ready to use: excess moisture encourages leafy greens to rot. • Refrigerate in the bottom drawer, in reusable zip-top bags. • Freeze and use in smoothies and sauces.	• Remove kale leaves from the stems; thinly slice or chop the stems. • With Swiss chard, the colourful stem is often delicate; chop or thinly slice the stems.
Herbs	• Rinse with water and dry thoroughly, then refrigerate in the bottom drawer. • Tender herbs (basil, chives, coriander, dill, mint, parsley etc): if you're using them within a day, no need to refrigerate, just snip off the bottom of the stems, remove any wilted or brown leaves, and place them in a jar or container with 2–3cm of water. • Blend tender herbs with a little water and freeze in an ice cube tray.	• The stems of tender herbs offer subtle flavour to many dishes. Chop the stems and add at the start of any sauté; finely chop or blitz to use in sauces.
Apples and pears	• Keep apples in the fruit bowl for up to a week; to store for longer, refrigerate in a paper bag in the bottom drawer. • Pears, if underripe, can be kept at room temperature; once soft, use immediately or stash them in the fridge for a day or two. • Squeeze a bit of citrus juice on exposed pieces of fruit, to prevent them from browning too quickly. • Keep away from bananas.	• I never peel my apples, but if you do, you can use the peel to infuse water or fruity drinks. • Cut apple or pear in half and scoop out the seeds.

	How to Store	**How to Prep to Avoid Waste**
Mushrooms	• Store in the fridge in their original packaging or a paper bag for up to one week, but use as soon as possible.	• Use the entire mushroom, no need to peel the skin or remove the stems. Wipe off any dirt or give them a quick rinse, then use immediately.
Bananas	• Cool place, out of direct sunlight. Don't refrigerate. • Fully ripe bananas – if not eaten straight away – should be peeled, sliced and frozen in an airtight zip-top bag. • Squeeze a bit of citrus juice on exposed pieces of bananas, to prevent them from browning too quickly. • Keep separate from apples, avocados, and other fruits.	• If you dare, the skin is edible. Scrape away the fleshy bit on the inside of the skin, using a spoon. Thinly slice the skin and fry with onions and garlic in stews or curries or make my BLT (page 241).
Citrus fruits	• Store at cool room temperature for up to a week, or refrigerate to prolong their shelf life. • Refrigerate slices or half-cut fruit.	• Scrub the skins. • If waxed, you can soak them for a few minutes in a bowl of hot water and vinegar, then scrub to remove the wax coating. • If a recipe asks for zest and juice, zest the fruit first – it's a lot easier to zest when the fruit is whole. • To use the whole fruit, slice in half, remove the pips then blend and freeze in ice cube trays (page 252).
Milk	• You can freeze milk. Pour into ice cube trays and use the frozen milk for smoothies, milkshakes or in iced coffee.	• N/A
Yoghurt	• Refrigerate on a lower shelf – not the fridge door. • Once opened, consume within 3–5 days. • Freezer friendly.	• N/A
Ginger	• Refrigerate in a reusable bag, in the bottom drawer.	• Wash if needed; no need to peel before grating or chopping.

How to Get the Best Out of Your Food!

	How to Store	**How to Prep to Avoid Waste**
Pasta	• Once opened, store dry, uncooked pasta in a cool, dry place for up to one year. Label and date, if necessary. I keep my pasta in an airtight container. • Fresh pasta: refrigerate and use by the use-by date. • Freeze unopened fresh pasta in its original packaging for up to six months.	• N/A
Bread	• Cool, dry area: a bread bin is ideal. • Store in a paper bag, not plastic – plastic creates moisture and encourages mould. • Don't refrigerate and don't store on top of your fridge – this can speed up mould growth. • If you're not going to eat the bread within three days, slice and freeze – or freeze half the loaf as soon as you bring it home. • Blitz stale bread and freeze as breadcrumbs.	• N/A
Rice	• Store uncooked rice in a cool, dry place in an airtight container to keep out moisture. Use within 12–24 months. • To store cooked rice, spread it on a clean, lightly oiled baking sheet to cool evenly. Transfer the cooled rice to an airtight container or reusable bag; press the air out of the bag before sealing. • Reheat cooked rice over medium heat for 2–5 minutes (depending on quantity) until thoroughly hot. • To freeze cooked rice, cool and store in the same way. Use within six months.	• Add rice to a large bowl and wash with cold water. Drain the water, add fresh cold water and rinse again, repeating several times until the water is clear and not cloudy. • This removes some of the starches and helps the rice cook more quickly.

Index

Occasion
Index

Pasta

Summer picnics or BBQ

Sweet

Notes

Acknowledgements

A lot of incredible women are behind this book.

Thank you to my literary agent Rachel Mills, who was a big supporter of my work way before we even started working together. It almost feels as though fate brought us together! I absolutely love working with you and feel so grateful for your honesty and dedication, and for always finding the time for me.

Thank you to Lizzy Gray. You are a powerhouse. Thank you, Sam Crisp, Alice King and the entire Ebury team who had their heads, hands, eyes and tastebuds involved in the making of this book. Thank you for steering *You Can Cook This!* in the best possible direction.

Lizzie Mayson, you are a ray of sunshine. Thank you for capturing the essence of my food and ethos in every single photo. Your photography is out of this world and I can't wait to continue working with you.

Thank you, Elena and Esther, for your help developing these recipes and for styling them so beautifully. Without you and your brilliant team, this book wouldn't be anywhere near as delicious. The recipes are foolproof and so are YOU!

Thank you to my online community. Without your support this book simply wouldn't exist. I don't want to get too gushy, but you really have changed my life and I will never take it for granted.

Lastly, I'd like to thank my wife Venetia – my sous chef, personal food critic and love. Thank you for challenging me to think in new ways and for guiding me in the best possible way. I'll always be here to cook you whatever you want. You truly are my favourite person to eat with and nothing feels more like home to me than you (and a bowl of pasta).

1

Ebury Press an imprint of Ebury Publishing,
20 Vauxhall Bridge Road,
London SW1V 2SA

Ebury Press is part of the Penguin Random House group of companies whose
addresses can be found at global.penguinrandomhouse.com

The authorised representative in the EEA is Penguin Random House Ireland, Morrison
Chambers, 32 Nassau Street, Dublin D02 YH68.

First published by Ebury Press in 2023
www.penguin.co.uk

A CIP catalogue record for this book is available from the British Library

Design: Evi-O.Studio | Evi O. & Emi Chiba

ISBN 9781529148800

Printed and bound in China by C&C Offset Printing Co., Ltd

Penguin Random House is committed to a sustainable future for
our business, our readers and our planet. This book is made from
Forest Stewardship Council® certified paper.